NINJA
Skills

NINJA
Skills

The Authentic Ninja
Training Manual

Antony
Cummins

WATKINS
Sharing Wisdom Since 1893

NINJA SKILLS
ANTONY CUMMINS

First published in the UK and USA in 2018 by
Watkins, an imprint of Watkins Media Limited
19 Cecil Court
London WC2N 4EZ

enquiries@watkinspublishing.com

Development Editor: Fiona Robertson
Editor: James Hodgson
Head of Design: Glen Wilkins
Production: Uzma Taj

A CIP record for this book is available from the British Library

ISBN: 978-1-78678-062-1

10 9 8 7 6 5 4 3 2 1

Typeset in Adobe Garamond Pro
Colour reproduction by XY Digital
Printed in China

www.watkinspublishing.com

"One who acts on principles, that is what a ninja should be."

Bansenshūkai, Fujibayashi-sensei, 1676

Contents

A NOTE ON TERMINOLOGY

The term ninja is correctly interpreted as *shinobi no mono* (*shinobi* carries the connotation of "hiding" and *mono* means "person"). This is often contracted to *shinobi*. The skill of *ninjutsu* is correctly spoken as *shinobi no jutsu*, "the arts of the *shinobi*". These are the terms used in the historical scrolls on which this book is based and so these are the terms used here.

Introduction

THE WORLD OF THE SHINOBI

Spanning a millennium, from the 9th to the 19th century, the age of the samurai was a glorious chapter in the chronicle of Japan. The samurai observed a refined and precise etiquette in all their activities, from the taking of tea to the taking of enemy heads. This emphasis on the "right way" of doing things continues to exert a powerful influence in modern Japanese culture.

Nestled within a samurai force, yet standing apart from it, lurked the shadowy *shinobi*, the infamous ninja agent. He was the commando, the spy, the betrayer. While "standard" samurai found lying and cheating repugnant, the *shinobi* were not bound by such scruples. They too followed an ethical code, but they considered duplicity to be acceptable as long as it was used in the service of their lord. The *shinobi* soldier would often integrate himself within the enemy, sharing in the rhythms of everyday life and steadily gaining their trust but all the while hiding a malign intent. He was a foul demon obeying the bidding of his gods, enabling the plans of his lord to bear fruit.

WHO WERE THE SHINOBI?

The *shinobi* were spy-commandos with multiple specialisms, all of which involved clandestine activity. These included espionage, counter-intelligence, surveillance, scouting, infiltration, propaganda, incendiary warfare and physical protection, as well as the capturing of any person targeted for arrest by the lord. An essential part of any Japanese military force, the *shinobi* were considered by many chroniclers as the "eyes and ears" of an army.

BELOW: Image of a thief by Edo-period artist, Hokusai.

Unlike the samurai, which was a specific social class, the *shinobi* was a paid military role that could be fulfilled by a soldier of any background. Many *shinobi* were from the samurai class, but others were simple *ashigaru* foot soldiers. Others still were itinerant monks, actors or tradesmen who might take on a temporary assignment. True *shinobi* owed their allegiance to a single lord, whether for the length of a short-term contract or across generations. Being a *shinobi* did not automatically confer any particular status; there were lower-grade *shinobi* as well as masters of the art (see lessons 18 and 19).

The *shinobi* were first recorded in the 14th century. They are believed to have become particularly influential during the turbulent Sengoku period (1467–*c*.1603), when Japan was in a near-constant state of civil war. They then fell into relative obscurity during the more stable Edo period (*c*.1603–1868), when the country was largely united under the Tokugawa shogunate. By the time of the Meiji Restoration in 1868, when imperial rule returned in place of military government, the historical *shinobi* and samurai had died out.

ABOUT THIS BOOK

Ninja Skills investigates the beliefs, tactics and practices of the Japanese *shinobi*. It draws directly from historical manuscripts, most of which date from the 17th century and were compiled by forward-thinking writers determined to record for future generations the experiences of *shinobi* who had served during the warring Sengoku period. The chief source for the 150 lessons contained within these pages is the 1676 manual the *Bansenshūkai*, written by Fujibayashi Yasutake. This has been supplemented by quotations and variations from other important works of the period, including the *Shōninki* by Natori Masazumi (Issui-sensei), the *Yōkan* series by Chikamatsu Shigenori, and the *Gunpō Jiyōshū* by Ogasawara Saku'un Katsuzo.

The lessons build on the original material to explain how, as a modern reader, you can interact with these skills. Commentaries expand upon each teaching, outlining the social, cultural and religious context and practical applications, in order to deepen your understanding of *shinobi no jutsu*. It is hoped that you will be able to incorporate some of the skills and insights into your own *shinobi* study. However, the world of the *shinobi* was very different from ours and some of the practices described are dangerous or illegal or both, and should not be emulated.

The teachings have been selected from all volumes of the *Bansenshūkai* and represent a broad overview of the writing of Fujibayashi-sensei. If you wish to delve more deeply into the source material, the appendices at the back of this book go into further detail about the scrolls and the Chinese military classics on which some of them are based. You can also read an English translation of the full *Bansenshūkai* in *The Book of Ninja* (Watkins, 2013).

The
Lessons

Fundamental Concepts

Lesson 1

THE PATH OF THE SHINOBI

"In our country we use the ideogram shinobi 忍 *as it has a deep meaning. Without realizing the meaning you will find it difficult to take even the first step on this path."*

Bansenshūkai, Fujibayashi-sensei, 1676

Those who wish to take the path of the *shinobi* must first understand the concepts represented by the *shinobi* ideogram. It carries the following essential meanings: "perseverance", "forbearance", "endurance", "secrecy" and "stealth". Through its use by agents engaged in espionage the ideogram has also come to have the connotations of "spy", "secret agent", "thief" and "infiltrator".

In the *Bansenshūkai* Fujibayashi-sensei explains that the *shinobi* ideogram comprises the characters for "heart" (心) and "blade" (刃), because to plunge themselves deep into the core of the enemy *shinobi* must forge their hearts into weapons that are hard and sharp like a blade.

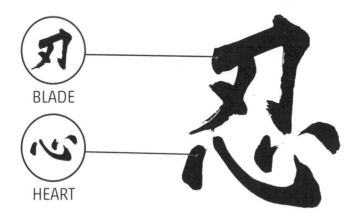

BLADE

HEART

ABOVE: A breakdown of the individual characters that make up the *shinobi* ideogram.

17

This is not a path for the weak. To venture into the dominion of the *shinobi* requires enormous self-control and a level of commitment and endurance that most people cannot attain.

What makes the path so difficult is that *shinobi* must be simultaneously loyal to their own clan and treacherous toward the enemy. They live within samurai society but remain in its shadow, forever close to the centre but always cast to the outside, as any betrayal could mean the downfall of a clan. Consequently, *shinobi* sit outside the lord's "light" but close enough to feel its "warmth". Unlike the average soldier, they do not benefit from the army's protection – they do not march within the ranks or camp behind sturdy palisades. The *shinobi* venture out before all others, alone, and put themselves in danger deep inside the adversary's stronghold.

ABOVE: Ideograms representing *shinobi no jutsu* ("the arts of the *shinobi*") by Monk Jyuhō Yamamoto.

Lesson 2

THE ORIGIN OF THE UNIVERSE

The Taoist creation myth heavily influences samurai and *shinobi* thought. According to the myth, before the universe existed there was a formless expanse called Wu-chi ("Pre-Universe"), which evolved into T'ai-chi ("The Great Ultimate"). The Great Ultimate then differentiated into negative and positive elements called *yin* and *yang*. While being contrary to each other, *yin* and *yang* also complement each other – a duality found in, for example, male and female, light and dark, and fire and water.

Yin and *yang* divide into "heaven, earth and man" (*tenchijin*), which exists in the four seasons of spring, summer, autumn and winter. This is the foundation for the five elements of Earth (*do*), Fire (*ka*), Metal (*gon*), Water (*sui*) and Wood (*moku*). The five elements give rise to the eight trigrams: Heaven (*qian*), Lake (*dui*), Fire (*li*), Thunder (*zhen*), Wind (*xun*), Water (*kan*), Mountain (*gen*) and Earth (*kun*). They in turn generate the whole world.

Yin and *yang* are also earth and heaven. When the body dies, *yin* and *yang* separate: the *yin* element – the body – crumbles and returns to the earth, while the *yang* element – the spirit – returns to heaven. Therefore, death is not an end but the beginning of another phase of life. This understanding is what enables the *shinobi* to face death without fear.

Shinobi skill: Do not mix up the Chinese version of the five elements shown above, known as the *gogyō* (五行), and the Indian version, known as the *gorin* (五輪).

RIGHT: The hierarchy of the Taoist universe.

Pre-Universe
⌄
The Great Ultimate
⌄
Positive and Negative
⌄
Heaven, Earth and Man
⌄
Spring, Summer, Autumn and Winter
⌄
Earth, Fire, Metal, Water and Wood
⌄
The Eight Trigrams
⌄
The Created Universe

Lesson 3

OF HEAVEN, EARTH AND MAN

The concept of *tenchijin* – "heaven, earth and man" – signifies the oneness of the universe. The Confucianist sage Mencius said that to govern a country you must take into account the time of heaven, the advantages of earth, and the harmony of man. The Natori-Ryū samurai tradition breaks these elements down as follows:

Time of heaven
- the date (important in divination)
- the 12-sign zodiac system
- the 10 celestial signs
- auspicious and inauspicious directions
- the energy of each season (important in divination)

Advantages of earth
- distant or close
- steep or flat
- large or small
- life and death

Harmony of man
- the unity of all people of all classes

Generals planning for a battle or *shinobi* preparing for a mission will greatly increase their chances of success if they understand this triad and align heaven, earth and man in their favour.

Lesson 4

SKILLS OF THE DARK AND SKILLS OF THE LIGHT

In the *Bansenshūkai* Fujibayashi-sensei divides the arts of the *shinobi* according to *yin* and *yang*. The *yin* aspect, the "dark side", is called *in* (陰), and the *yang* aspect, the "light side", is called *yō* (陽). Any skill (jutsu) found in the arts of the *shinobi* is either *in-jutsu*, a "skill of the dark", or *yō-jutsu*, a "skill of the light". *Shinobi* themselves are also classified along these lines, as *in-nin* (陰忍), "*shinobi* of the dark", and *yō-nin* (陽忍), "*shinobi* of the light". Typically, *in-nin* move in stealth like commandos, whereas *yō-nin* use deception and disguise to "hide in plain sight" like spies.

Yin In	Yang Yō
Earth	Heaven
Darkness	Light
Water	Fire
Female	Male
Stillness	Movement

Practical examples of *in-jutsu* include travelling out of sight over mountains and away from roads, moving in stealth around enemy positions at night, cutting through walls and infiltrating buildings, and entering in secret without ever being seen. In contrast, *yō-jutsu* might involve disguising yourself as a local tradesman, using the local dialect and moving freely among the enemy, all the while counting forces, making maps and surveying building layouts. Alternatively, you might settle on the edge of an enemy town before a conflict starts and become familiar with the townsfolk. Then when war breaks out, because you are already known to the enemy, you will not be suspected of being an agent. Another example of *yō-jutsu* is placing a female spy-maid (*kunoichi*) within an enemy household.

MIXING IN AND YŌ

Lower-level *shinobi* should complete a mission using only *in-jutsu* or *yō-jutsu*. However, more experienced agents will know when it is appropriate to switch between the two. Such an agent might enter into an enemy castle by using stolen passwords or pretending to be the servant of a local samurai (*yō-jutsu*). They will then pick the correct time to infiltrate in secret, climbing or breaking through into the most secure areas (*in-jutsu*).

Alternatively, seasoned *shinobi* might infiltrate a samurai house in stealth (*in-jutsu*) and then hold a false conversation with themselves to mislead any guards who overhear (*yō-jutsu*) so that they can continue infiltrating deeper (*in-jutsu*). Or they might place a *kunoichi* in the enemy household (*yō-jutsu*) and have her open the doors at night so that they can infiltrate (*in-jutsu*). Fujibayashi-sensei calls this switching of skills *yō-chū in jutsu* (陽中陰術) – the "skills of darkness inside light".

Lesson 5

THE CONCEPT OF INSUBSTANTIAL AND SUBSTANTIAL

Kyojitsu (虚実) is a concept that you need to understand, as it is the basis of the *shinobi* mindset. Meaning "that which is insubstantial", *kyo* (虚) carries connotations of falseness, emptiness, untruth, deception, weakness and unpreparedness. On the other hand, *jitsu* (実) means "that which is substantial" and represents truth, fullness, correctness, honesty, strength and preparedness. The art of the *shinobi* lies in telling the difference between the two qualities.

ABOVE: The fan is substance; the shadow of the fan is insubstantiality.

In the image above, the fan is substantial and true, while the shadow of the fan is insubstantial and untrue. It may look like a fan, but it is only a projection, an illusion. We can apply this concept to warfare. If a military force places 1,000 men on the field of battle, a good strategist will ask whether this is truly the whole force (*jitsu*). Or has the enemy hidden 2,000 additional men, waiting to ambush? If so, that is a false appearance designed to mislead, a shadow of the truth (*kyo*).

Similarly, *shinobi* working undercover to gather intelligence from the enemy must always question whether the information they have received is true or whether in fact it is false, deliberately planted by the enemy in order to misguide.

The concept of *kyojitsu* is deep and profound and is a fundamental part of *shinobi no jutsu*. Without mastering this idea an espionage agent can never become a *jōnin* – an expert *shinobi* (see lesson 19).

Lesson 6

WAITING FOR THE ENEMY TO MAKE A MOVE

"There is no difference between the principles for ninjutsu *(espionage) and the principles for* kenjutsu *(swordsmanship). When your opponent is not going to strike at you with their sword, it is difficult for you to strike at them. Instead you should strike at the moment that the opponent attacks. The same holds true in* ninjutsu: *when the enemy is in a state of non-movement, you should not move either. Infiltrate at the exact moment that the enemy moves."*

Bansenshūkai, Fujibayashi-sensei, 1676

Fujibayashi's comparison illuminates one of the core principles of espionage. When your opponent in a sword fight is in a defensive position they are like a sealed castle, difficult to attack. But when they make an attacking move they have to open up their defences, which is something you can exploit. The key is to find the opponent's weak spot before their attack does you harm.

The *shinobi* has to either bring about movement in the enemy position or wait for the enemy to move of their own accord. When the enemy moves they give the *shinobi* a chance to infiltrate unnoticed, but if the enemy is inactive, any movement by the *shinobi* becomes obvious to the defenders.

RIGHT: An example of movement in swordsmanship.

Lesson 7

THE THREE DISEASES OF THE SHINOBI

"The three diseases of shinobi no jutsu *are to fear, to take the enemy too lightly and to think too much."*

Bansenshūkai, Fujibayashi-sensei, 1676

FEAR

OVERTHINKING

UNDERESTIMATION

FEAR

"If you cannot detach yourself from death, then you will fear everything. It is said that nothing is a greater change than your own death, think on this. This is the same as to stop breathing though a fear of ageing."

Heika Jōdan, Issui-sensei, c.1670

Left to run amok, fear – particularly fear of death – can paralyse your thoughts. The 20th-century science fiction writer Frank Herbert famously wrote, "Fear is the mind-killer." This statement carries a universal truth, which resonates through the ages.

To have no fear is recklessness; to have too much fear is cowardice. *Shinobi* need to identify the fear in their mind and take control of it.

UNDERESTIMATION

A devastating mistake that strategists can make is to consider their enemy to be stupid or beneath them. An adversary is a human and all humans have different types of intelligence. You may consider your opponent to be lacking in the kind of intelligence you possess, but their kind of intelligence may find a way to see through your tactics. Furthermore, do not forget that the enemy forces will contain multiple opponents, each with a different kind and level of intelligence. Therefore, always view the enemy as a skilled and accomplished nemesis and make plans accordingly. Never allow your strategies to become entrenched in complexity, but also never lower the standards of intellect and reasoning in your planning.

OVERTHINKING

Each situation we encounter has a central point surrounded by an imaginary boundary and beyond this boundary lies another situation. Often in martial arts you may ask your opponent, "What if I do this?" to which the opponent's response is, "I would do this," to which you say, "Then what if I do this?" and the chain of change continues. At this point the original situation no longer exists and both people have found themselves in new circumstances.

The same happens when a *shinobi* plans a strategy for a clandestine operation. What if the enemy does this? What if they do that? What if they do something else? There is a central point, which is the problem, the here and now, and within this situation there are foreseeable eventualities. When your thoughts push beyond these possibilities they create a chain of change and eventually the situation is changed beyond the actual truth. In fact, the situation is still the same, it has changed only in your mind.

A good *shinobi* will know the difference between a reasonable level of contingency planning and over-speculation.

Lesson 8

DRAWING FROM DIFFERENT RELIGIONS

The samurai class existed for approximately one millennium, from the 9th century to the 19th century, and during this time a variety of belief systems became prominent in Japan. Each of these influenced samurai and *shinobi* philosophy, although individual warriors would have been subject to their own beliefs and the political climate of the time. Here we give a brief overview of the most significant religions. To gain a fuller understanding of the *shinobi* mindset you should venture deeper into these teachings.

The Principal Religions of Japan

Buddhism and Zen
Confucianism
Shinto and Folklore
Taoism

BUDDHISM

Founded in India in around the fifth century BC by Siddhartha Gautama, Buddhism teaches us the Four Noble Truths, which are:

1 Life contains suffering.
2 Desire or "thirst" for certain impermanent states or things produces suffering, which in turn leads to a build-up of *karma*, tying us to the endless cycle of death and rebirth.
3 If we identify and overcome our desire, we will reduce our suffering and *karma*.
4 Inner peace is found by cultivating a correct mind.

By cultivating a correct mind, we can liberate ourselves from the cycle of death and rebirth. We do this by following the Noble Eightfold Path:

1   correct view – understanding the nature of reality
2   correct intention – acting from compassion
3   correct speech – communicating in a non-harmful way
4   correct conduct – not exploiting others
5   correct livelihood – pursuing a non-harmful occupation
6   correct effort – conducting accurate self-analysis and adjusting accordingly
7   correct mindfulness – continuing to perfect awareness of all things
8   correct meditation – developing the ability to live in the moment

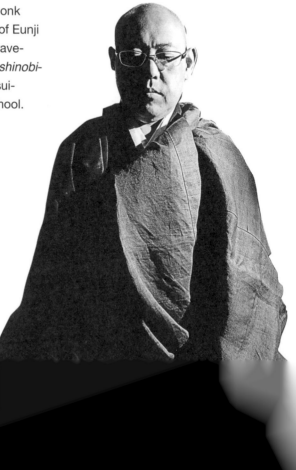

RIGHT:Japanese Buddhist monk Jyuhō Yamamoto, overseer of Eunji Temple in Wakayama and grave-keeper for the 17th-century *shinobi*-master Natori Masazumi (Issui-sensei) of the Natori-Ryū school.

Early Buddhism	Zen
Reciting the Sutras	Meditation
Magic rituals	To clear the mind
Worship of the various Buddhas	To understand the mind of the Buddha

ABOVE: The basic distinction between Buddhism and Zen.

A particular school of Buddhism known as Zen, which focuses above all on meditation, came to Japan in the 12th century. Zen Buddhism became popular among the samurai, who found that the mental discipline they developed through intensive Zen meditation enhanced their martial arts skills and helped them to face the enemy in battle without fear of death.

CONFUCIANISM

Confucianism is the study of the ways and teachings of the revered Chinese philosopher Confucius (551–479 BC). It centres on developing a harmonious relationship between the individual (microcosm) and society (macrocosm). Confucius teaches us to cultivate certain virtues, such as benevolence, righteousness, loyalty, and respect for ritual, family and tradition. All members of a society have a collective responsibility to develop these virtues within themselves, in order to serve the common good. Confucianism became particularly influential in Japan toward the end of the 17th century. It is not hard to see how its ethic of unswerving loyalty and selflessness regulated by an ever-vigilant mind can be applied to the *shinobi* path.

SHINTŌ

Shintō ("path of the gods") collects together various Japanese folk religions. Central to Shintō are Japan's native gods, or *kami* (神), who reside in the natural world. Adherents worship at a shrine where areas of purity are marked off by *shimenawa* ropes and the iconic *torii* gates. Inside the shrine is the focus of veneration, which is normally a rock known as an *iwakura* (磐座)

or a mirror called a *kagami* (鏡). The latter is often referenced in traditional martial literature as a symbol for the mind. Like a mirror, the mind reflects the world around it. If the mind-mirror is unpolished, warped or dusty then the reflection of reality will be distorted and false. Therefore, *shinobi* constantly "polish" their mind so that their understanding of reality is clear and pure.

TAOISM

The ancient Chinese tradition of Taoism is not found as a full or formal religion in Japan, but, as we have seen already, elements of Taoist philosophy, such as the concepts of *yin* and *yang*, saturate Japanese culture.

In Japanese culture it is acceptable to draw different insights from different beliefs, rather than subscribing exclusively to one. For example, the agricultural reformer and sage Ninomiya Sontoku (1787–1856) considered Shintō as the basis for the country, Confucianism as the basis for the governing of the country and Buddhism as the basis for the governing of the mind. He even broke this blend down into set proportions: a half Shintō, a quarter Confucianism and a quarter Buddhism.

Lesson 9

RESPECT FOR HEAVEN

"Those in a high seat of power are nothing compared with the gods of heaven. If you offend the gods, then you have none to whom you can pray."
Bansenshūkai, Fujibayashi-sensei, 1676

Shinobi live in a world of lies and deception, but that does not mean they should be dishonest. They are agents contracted to serve a clan. While they perform evil deeds in this role, *shinobi* must maintain the strictest of moral codes in their inner life, believe in the gods, practise sincerity, cultivate their mind and follow the Way (see lesson 10). For if they do not do this they will fall into despair and lose the support of the gods.

Lesson 10

FOLLOWING THE WAY

"The Way is indescribable."

Lao-Tzu (604–531 BC), reputed author of the Tao Te Ching

The Way is the central concept of Taoism. It is considered as the power behind the construction and governing of the universe; it is outside of time and space yet it permeates all existence. Like the Western concept of God, the Way is unknowable. However, God is commonly personified as a man whereas the Way has no identity, no gender, no number.

How then to follow the Way, if it is unknowable? If any answer to this question can be found it will be in the teachings of the Tao Te Ching, the defining work of Taoist philosophy. Observe the principle of *wu-wei*, or *mui* (無為) as it is known in Japanese: do not force the situation, flow with the moment (see lesson 147).

Note the difference between *the* Way and a way, such as:

- *chadō* (茶道) – the way of the tea ceremony
- *shodō* (書道) – the way of calligraphy
- *kadō* (華道) – the way of flower arrangement
- *kōdō* (香道) – the way of fragrance

These are all ancient traditions that can help you to concentrate the mind and lead a life of harmony.

Lesson 11

MAINTAINING A CORRECT MIND

At the beginning of the *Bansenshūkai* Fujibayashi-sensei introduces the concept of *seishin*, the correct mindset – from *sei* (正) "correct" and *shin* (心) "mind". Humans are extremely logical creatures and will follow a series of steps until they arrive at a conclusion. This is known as deductive reasoning. For example, the hill slopes downwards and therefore a ball will roll down it. However, often people begin their reasoning from an incorrect starting point, which leads to myriad misunderstandings, misuses and malpractices. Fujibayashi-sensei teaches us that before training as *shinobi* we should cultivate *seishin* to help us understand what is correct and what is not correct, what is truth and what is falsehood. Only then will our minds will bloom in the correct direction.

SEISHIN
CORRECT MIND

HONSHIN
ORIGINAL MIND

Lesson 12

THE WAY OF THE SHINOBI IS HONESTY

Paradoxically for an agent of deception and lies, the way of the *shinobi* is to be completely honest. Many of the teachings concerning the *shinobi* qualify this simple instruction by describing three aspects of truth.

ASPECT 1

A *shinobi* who has been set up undercover needs to develop a reputation for honesty. If you become known as a trustworthy person, then when the time comes you can place a lie that will bring down the enemy clan.

ASPECT 2

If you stray onto the path of dishonesty and greed, then money and power can weaken your resolve and you will become susceptible to manipulation. You could end up as a double agent or a rogue agent who swaps sides depending on which gives you the most benefit.

ASPECT 3

To be a *shinobi* you must be clear about the workings of the human mind and understand your own psychology. Most of us believe that our point of view is correct and we do not understand the effect our emotions have on our thoughts and actions. Once you understand the workings of your mind you will become internally honest, meaning that you can identify when your mind is overpowering or manipulating you (see lesson 145). Then you will understand not only yourself but also the enemy.

ABOVE: A samurai is straight and true, inside and out.

ABOVE: The core of a *shinobi* is true, but outside are lies and deception.

ABOVE: The *nusubito* thief is crooked inside and out.

Lesson 13

BE LIKE WATER

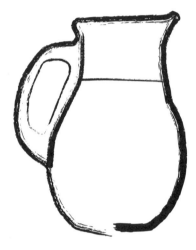

There is an old Chinese teaching: "Water adjusts itself to the vessel it is in." When water is put into a teapot it takes the shape of the teapot, when in a cup it takes the shape of the cup, etc. Similarly, we change our behaviour and personality to suit the environment around us. Issui-sensei of the Natori-Ryū school tells us that when we interact with a merchant or someone who values money, then we, too, shall become more fascinated with wealth; or if we see someone we find attractive, then we will have lustful thoughts. These are examples of how "water adjusts to the vessel it is in."

Those who take the path of the *shinobi* may find themselves in extreme situations involving bribery, extortion, lying, thieving, killing and so on. Their entire lifestyle will become one of manipulation and maleficence. Therefore, they need to take full control and understand how to protect their character from external experiences.

In some respects you will need to "be like water" – in adapting yourself to your environment so that you do not attract attention – but you must also ensure that the demands of your role do not twist your true nature.

Lesson 14

THE TREASURE OF FIRE AND WATER

Fire can fill a room with warmth and good cheer, cool water can be "liquid gold" to a thirsty traveller, but in the wrong circumstances they can kill you. Likewise, the arts of the *shinobi* can bring great benefits to a lord or they can destroy them and their house.

Leaders must understand the arts of the *shinobi* so that they can place their pieces "on the board" in the correct way. They must have multiple *shinobi* – some of whom are unaware of each other's true identity – reporting back to them so that they can compile an accurate account of enemy movements. This is done so that any *shinobi* who are reporting different information from the others can be identified as double agents. Without such measures, false reports flow back up the chain of command, double agents find their way into a leader's confidence and secret plans become known to the enemy. Therefore, like fire and water, *shinobi* can be either a treasure or a hazard, bringing either bounty or destruction.

LEFT: Fire and water can both be either saviour or assassin, so must be treated with respect.

Lesson 15

WORKING OUTSIDE THE SYSTEM

The *shinobi* straddle two worlds, the public and the private. Just like MI5, MI6, the CIA, SAS, SBS and the Navy Seals, we know they exist but their agents, objectives and operations are secret.

Surprisingly, many people may have been able to identify a *shinobi* in historical Japan. The military writer Chikamatsu Shigenori (1695–1778) tells us that warlords would have *shinobi* who were known to the world (*yō no shinobi*) and secret agents whose identity was kept secret (*in no shinobi*). In the Sengoku period (1467–*c*.1603) some *shinobi* were hidden within the enemy while others moved with the main army. They were billeted separately but could be seen as *shinobi*. It is also known that in the Edo period (*c*.1603–1868), some *shinobi* wore a specific jacket and crests while on duty and engaged in training, meaning that everyone in the castle and castle town knew who they were, but also that others were kept secret, ready to do the lord's bidding.

Students of the *shinobi* arts must have a thorough understanding of general samurai skills, from physical martial arts through to military tactics. They must hold *shinobi no jutsu* as an auxiliary art that they specialize in and develop themselves as an exclusive unit above others, no matter whether their identity as a *shinobi* is open to the public or kept hidden from all but a few.

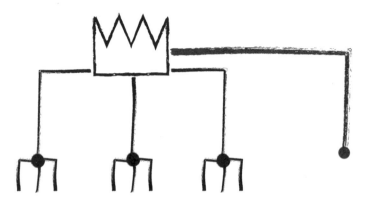

ABOVE: A *shinobi* is outside of the system.

Lesson 16

BEING THE EYES AND EARS OF THE ARMY

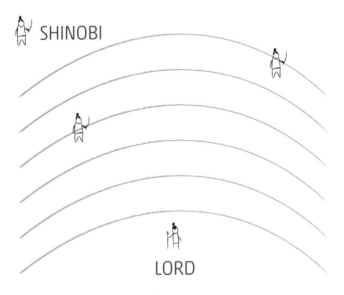

SHINOBI

LEFT: A *shinobi* works outside a lord's observation.

LORD

Whether during times of war or times of peace, the *shinobi's* task is always to serve as the eyes and ears of the lord. When a lord resides within his own castle he can "see" only to the borders of his lands, likewise when an army is on the march it can "see" only to the crest of the next hill.

The first wave of reconnaissance are called *monomi* scouts. However, for deeper observation the *shinobi* move outside the range of the castle and the army, relaying information back to the lord on the situation beyond the borders of the land. They are the eyes and ears of the lord beyond his normal field of information. Furthermore, the *shinobi* will observe those inside the boundaries and bring information about the lord's own forces. This is also the responsibility of the *metsuke*, internal observers who watch for any conspirators from within.

Shinobi skill: *Shinobi* must observe both friends and enemies, as friends often become enemies in times of war and change. It is the job of the *shinobi* to act as inspectors within their own ranks.

Lesson 17

SHINOBI OUTFITS

Perhaps the best answer to the question of what a *shinobi* should wear? is that it depends on the situation. What you should definitely not wear is a hooded black "ninja suit", as this is a modern invention. However, it may be appropriate to wear black, particularly when infiltrating at night.

When using *yō-jutsu* – disguise – the most important thing is to correctly mimic the target identity. However, the principle of disguise also has a place in *in-jutsu* – stealth. If *shinobi* are moving as a squad to infiltrate a castle during a siege, they may choose to wear partial armour and helmets, and carry spears.

LEFT: Different lengths of sleeve can traditionally mean different things in Japan. However, *shinobi* typically wear a classic *kimono* sleeve.

ABOVE: The *tasuki* is a piece of cloth used to tie the sleeves back when engaging in work of various types. *Shinobi* might tie their sleeves back when infiltrating or leave them open to give easy access to tools.

When moving into an enemy battle camp in an isolated area they might also wear the outfit shown on the previous page, but strap down or tighten all equipment so that it makes no sound, i.e. stop weapons from rattling, water flasks from sloshing, armour from jangling etc. Or when infiltrating a complex as a squad, *shinobi* may wear light-fitting clothes and no armour but carry weapons and use white cloths as headbands or other identification markers. However, when infiltrating alone they may be very lightly armed and wear only loose-fitting clothes, but when moving through rough terrain they may need more rugged clothing, such as furs in winter.

"Close scouts should wear various clothes of their own choice. When infiltrating in the daytime, they should wear normal street clothes so as not to be questioned by anyone. At night when investigating an area they should wear lightweight clothes that allow freedom of movement. When investigating forests and mountains they should wear clothes that allow them to run around with ease."

Murakami family traditions, 1639

A *kimono* allows the wearer to carry items easily on his person, inside the *kimono* breast, in the sleeve or in a small purse on the belt, which makes it a useful garment for a *shinobi*. The *Bansenshūkai* has several examples of the sleeve being used as a "pocket". However, the Inkō-Ryu school says to use a thin-sleeved jacket as shown below.

These are some general points about *shinobi* clothing. Later lessons will go into more detail about items of clothing for specific situations.

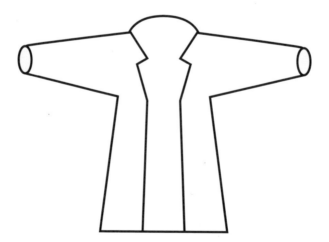

Lesson 18

SHINOBI RANKS

The modern concept of belts or grades does not exist in the *shinobi* arts. Traditionally, a *shinobi* was measured by his ability to perform his duties successfully. However, some ancient records, such as the *Bansenshūkai* and the *Taiheiki*, do give us a broad ranking system:

- *Jōnin* (上忍) – *shinobi* of the highest ability
- *Chūnin* (中忍) – *shinobi* of a middle-level ability
- *Genin* (下忍) – *shinobi* of lower ability

This system does not measure a *shinobi's* social status, it simply assesses the agent's ability to perform *ninjutsu*. A *jōnin* is an agent of exquisite skill, someone who is sent out on the most important missions and who deals with the most difficult situations (see lesson 19). *Chūnin* and *genin* are assigned lesser tasks. While they are still well-trained and better developed than the average member of the public – and maybe even the average soldier – they are yet to reach the heights of the *jōnin*.

Dating to the eighth century, the *menkyo* licensing system is another way to assess students of traditional Japanese arts, including *shinobi no jutsu*. In this system the highest level of licence is known as *menkyo kaiden* (免許皆伝). This is awarded only to the most accomplished practitioners.

上忍
JŌNIN

中忍
CHŪNIN

下忍
GENIN

Lesson 19

JŌNIN – THE PERFECT SHINOBI

A *jōnin* is considered the perfect ninja. As a *shinobi* student you should aspire to this status, although achieving it is another matter.

Fujibayashi-sensei details the qualities required to be a *jōnin*. You must demonstrate loyalty to your lord, the courage of a hero, strategic acumen and a record of achievement. Strong of body, you must nonetheless be gentle when not in action. You must have a keen sense of righteousness and an absence of desire and never forget what you owe to others. Your mental qualities should include fluency in speech and writing, an ability to think deeply and a fondness for learning principles and right action, and you must be difficult to deceive. You must know the morals of the samurai class and the ways of Japanese and Chinese ancient warriors. As well as military affairs, you should have knowledge of the various arts, including poetry, music and dance, have the ability to impersonate others and be proficient in many other disciplines. *Jōnin* are always dignified, honest and good, and should never be argumentative.

Spiritually, you must know heaven's will and understand Confucianism and Buddhism. Always be aware that life and death have their determined appointment and rise above your own self-interest while bearing the words of ancient sages in mind.

Your family will also come under scrutiny. Your spouse and other relatives should be of good descent to minimize the risk of any of them becoming a reversed spy.

You should be well travelled, study hard and learn deeply the art of *shinobi no jutsu* so as to achieve the highest level of understanding within it and gain merits in battle.

Lesson 20

THE SHINOBI INFILTRATION SQUAD

Though *shinobi* may work alone at times, they often collaborate in teams. All the group must work as a single and coherent unit but individual members have their own responsibilities. A *shinobi* squad recruited to infiltrate a samurai residence will typically consist of the following:

SHITE (仕手) – THE MAIN INFILTRATOR

The main infiltration agent is highly skilled, an expert in the arts of *shinobi no jutsu*. They use infiltration tools and work deep inside the enemy house and carry out the main objective of the mission.

SHITEZOE (仕手添) – SUPPORTERS TO THE MAIN INFILTRATOR

Like the main infiltration agent, *shitezoe* are among the most highly-skilled *shinobi*. They infiltrate alongside the main performer but branch off to report on the status of the enemy inside – whether they are asleep or on the move etc.

TSURONIN (通路人) – LIAISON

Tsuronin carry reports and instructions from the infiltrators deep inside the enemy complex to the agents outside, and vice versa.

AIZU MOCHI (相圖持) – SIGNAL-SENDERS

The communications branch of the team, they use *fūrin* (風鈴), a type of wind chime, and *shisoku-bi* (紙燭火), a paper candle, both of which are used to convey prearranged signals. *Aizu mochi* should be positioned for maximum visibility of the signals – more than one signal-sender may be needed.

HARI (張) – WATCHMEN

Hari take up position at specified locations and observe and raise the alarm if an enemy advances into their position. While this role can be performed by fully trained *shinobi*, it is often assigned to less experienced agents or anyone who may be considered a liability. Fujibayashi-sensei warns us that such people may run at the sight of their allies returning.

Also included within this category are exit guards, who are agents of a resolute nature. They are responsible for protecting the squad's withdrawal by locking doors, stretching out tripwires and scattering caltrops (ground spikes). They are also tasked with the slaying of any enemy who tries to follow in pursuit; they may need to move down the corridors, stabbing with their short swords, pushing all the inhabitants back into the inner section of the household.

PREPARATION, PASSWORDS AND IDENTIFICATION

The squad will decide on the passwords to be used (*aikotoba*) and each one should wear an identifying marker (*aijirushi*), such as a white headband or section of cloth somewhere on the body. Also, the group may decide to formulate a written oath, promising not to flee from the raid and to uphold the obligations of their position.

Infiltration Skills

Lesson 21

USING SOUND AS CAMOUFLAGE

Fujibayashi-sensei often uses the following phrase to describe how quiet a *shinobi* must be: "as though you are listening to frost fall on a cold night".

However, it is not always possible to work completely silently, so learn to use sound to cover your movements. If there are natural sounds such as running water, then these can be used to cover the noise of the *shinobi's* work (be aware, though, that experienced guards know to look for enemy infiltrators in such positions). Another option is to work at times when pervasive sounds such as wind and rain cover whole areas. This is why there is so much guidance in the *Bansenshūkai* and other manuals on forecasting wind and rain. These weathers will cover the inevitable noise of infiltration and cause less vigilant guards to take shelter. Understanding weather patterns and predicting wind and rain are fundamental skills for a *shinobi* agent.

ABOVE: *Shinobi* use sounds, such as hour bells, as signals to move and camouflage to cover the sound of their movements.

Lesson 22

LIGHT AND DARK PATROLS

When either defending or infiltrating a castle or battle camp, you must take into account the concept of light and dark patrols.

- A light patrol is a classic patrol made up of either a single person or a group who carry torches and inspect an area openly, illuminating any shadowy places.
- A dark patrol (*kamaritsuke*, "to discover *kamari* agents") is a secondary patrol who operate in stealth and without lights. They may be independent or follow after a light patrol.

When operating in a light patrol, make sure you know when and where the dark patrol is working so that you do not mistake them for the enemy. When you are in a dark patrol, make sure all members know the correct passwords so that no one can infiltrate in the darkness. Anyone moving in stealth and without a password should be considered an enemy *shinobi*. Think deeply on the concept of light and darkness when defending an area.

Shinobi **skill:** When defending a camp or fortress, deploy guards with torches, but after them send out guards without torches who sneak about in the dark to find enemy agents. When you are attacking, remember that when the guards with torches have passed other guards may be lurking in the dark.

ABOVE: A light patrol with a lamp and a stealthy dark patrol without.

Lesson 23

THE THREE STAGES OF CONCENTRATION

Any infiltration agent has to be aware of the three stages of concentration:

- the beginning – people are active, enthusiastic and eager
- the middle – people start to become slack-minded, lazy and uninterested
- the end – people are bored, eager to finish and move on

ABOVE: The three stages of concentration: alert, mind drifting and bored.

When infiltrating a position, *shinobi* should observe when the guards change and the length of the watch. That way they can time their infiltration for when the guard's concentration is likely to be flagging. The best times to infiltrate are when movement occurs within the target area or when guards become inattentive (concentration stage 3). Furthermore, people lose their concentration more quickly in extreme weather, such as in a downpour of rain, high winds or intense heat.

Shinobi **skill:** Know when an enemy guard has started to lose concentration. Plan your own watches so that guards change before they become weary.

51

Lesson 24

PREPARING FAKE LETTERS

ABOVE: A fake letter can be stitched into the collar in case of capture.

If you are captured during an infiltration you will need something to give you the upper hand. Fujibayashi-sensei recommends the idea of the false traitor. Before a mission of stealth pick one enemy general or military officer whom you think *could* be suspected of defecting, then write a letter containing a false agreement between your allies and the supposed defector and stitch the letter into your collar. If you are captured reveal this letter to your captors. This will knock the enemy off balance and turn all attention to the "traitor". They will be removed from their position while an investigation commences and, importantly, the enemy will almost certainly allow you to return to your side on condition that you carry false information back with you.

Issui-sensei has a variation on this strategy for use when infiltrating a civilian residence. He advises agents to carry a false love letter to a maid so that any captors will not mistake the *shinobi* for a thief. This is very important, as theft was punishable by death in medieval Japan.

***Shinobi* skill:** *Shinobi* must know what to do if they are captured. Good strategy includes preparing for the worst.

Lesson 25

WHISPER

THE SOFT NOISE TEST

One of the difficulties you will face when infiltrating is judging whether the guards in a dark, quiet guardroom are alert or inattentive (or even asleep). In this situation carry out a "soft noise test". One manual suggests throwing some small stones; another advises a whisper in the dark. On a wet night you could stick an open umbrella in the ground so that the patter of rain can be heard upon it. All of these tests should cause observant guards to stir at the sound and investigate,

ABOVE: The soft whisper test will help identify how alert a guard is.

which tells you that they are paying attention. However, be aware that some guards might lay a trap by pretending not to have heard the sound.

Shinobi **skill:** The soft noise test will confirm that guards are listening, but you cannot trust it to confirm they are *not* listening. Infiltration is a constant game of cat and mouse between *shinobi* and guard.

RIGHT: An example of the "umbrella in the rain" trick from a *shinobi* manual (modern copy in the Cummins Collection).

Lesson 26

PULLING UP TOOLS WITH A ROPE

This is an obvious use of rope, but a critical one. In *shinobi* squads a single agent scales a high fortification first, without any equipment to burden them, save for a rope which they lower down once they have reached the top. They can then haul up any equipment and the other *shinobi* can follow after it. There is no record of the knots used by the *shinobi*, but the illustration here shows a marling spike hitch which is used in the West for a similar task. Cloth or net bags can also be attached to the rope and filled with equipment.

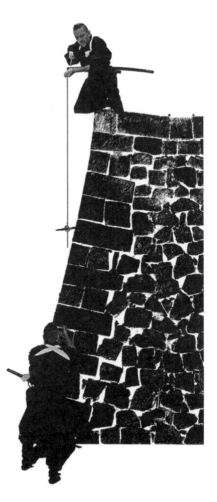

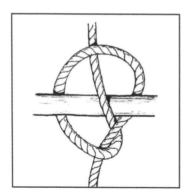

ABOVE: A marling spike hitch is a reliable knot to use when lifting tools with a rope.

Lesson 27

USING SCABBARDS FOR PROTECTION

The *shinobi* manuals contain surprisingly few physical fighting skills. The *Bansenshūkai* does not show how to perform techniques with the long and short swords (which samurai and *shinobi* typically carried), but it does demonstrate how to position your scabbards to avoid cuts. This is particularly important for *shinobi*, who will generally not burden themselves with armour when infiltrating. You should push your scabbards to each side and spin them into a vertical position. This will give you some protection at the sides from slashing moves. Understand it is quite probable that earlier Japanese swordsmanship focused on pull–push cuts and not over-dramatic swipes so the scabbards would act to stop slashes to the waist. Swordsmen would most likely have moved in a more closed fashion than is customary in modern martial arts and would have used shorter, harder slashes.

ABOVE: *Jōdan no kamae* – the high posture with two swords. Variations do exist with slightly different positioning of the swords.

Lesson 28

THE PULLING ROPE

With no moonlight for guidance, the passages between buildings in an enemy complex can be hard to navigate. Likewise, the rooms and corridors of a large house or fortification are often covered in a blanket of gloom. To overcome poor visibility a *shinobi* will use a long length of cord called a *hikinawa* (引縄), "pulling rope". Secure one end at the original point of infiltration and carry the rest coiled in your hand. As you creep around the target area, pay out the rope behind you, like Theseus in the Labyrinth. Then you will easily be able to follow the rope back out to your entry point. Such a cord is difficult for any patrol to see in the dark but enables you to exit efficiently in an emergency.

RIGHT: The *hikinawa* "pulling rope" is used to find an exit quickly when infiltrating an enemy compound at night.

Lesson 29

THE DIGGING TOOL

In modern Japanese animation, the *kunai* has become known as a throwable dagger-like weapon. However, evidence from ancient manuals shows that the *kunai* should be used as a tool, not a weapon. Measuring 30–50cm (12–20in) and ending in a heavy-duty narrow triangular spike, it may look like a

ABOVE: The *kunai* is used for digging or anchoring other objects.

dagger but it serves primarily as a robust digging implement or as a piton. Use it, for example, to dig out an entry channel below a fence, palisade or wall, or to anchor a rope bridge.

Lesson 30

SILENT SANDALS

Walking around in a house, particularly one with wooden floors, can be problematic. As well as the normal sound of footsteps, other dangers include squeaking

ABOVE: A pair of silent sandals with padded soles.

floorboards and wet footprints (if it has been raining). The *Bansenshūkai* and the secret teachings of Natori-Ryū recommend carrying "silent sandals" in the sleeve of your *kimono* to be worn once you have infiltrated a building. These should have padded soles made from a soft material. Interestingly, in World War II the British Special Operations Executive (SOE) also supplied its agents with padded footwear for use when breaking into a building.

Lesson 31

APPROACHING FROM THE LEEWARD SIDE

ABOVE: The agent on the right is on the leeward side of the enemy on the left.

The windward side is the side of an object that faces the wind, while the sheltered area is called the leeward side. For an agent infiltrating it is best to move into the wind – that is, toward the leeward side of your target – because this pushes the sound you make behind you and away from the enemy, while any sound that the enemy makes is carried on the wind toward you. This principle also applies to tell-tale smells, such as sweat, oils, gunpowder, etc.

Lesson 32

PLOTTING A QUIET ROUTE

When planning your route into a target area, avoid all elements that will make sounds, such as twigs, dried grass, water-logged areas, etc. Steer clear of bushes and other heavy foliage that you would have to fight your way through. Try to find an elevated position and observe the area as well as you can, taking note of the most promising approach routes. The weather is also of great importance: dry weather will make leaves and other natural debris crunch and crack underfoot,while rain dampens everything down, including sound.

Lesson 33

DISTRACTION TACTIC TO GET THROUGH A GATEWAY

Samurai houses were small compounds with a complex of buildings encircled by an external wall. The only legitimate way through the outer wall was a guarded gateway. This skill, found in the *Bansenshūkai* and in Natori-Ryū's teaching, enables a two- or three-person team of *shinobi* to lure the guard out into the open so that one of the agents can steal in.

1 Create a disturbance at the gate such as a false messenger or a false fight.
2 Once the guard responds lure them out as far away from the gate as possible.
3 With the guard's attention now focused away from the gate, a hidden agent can move through the gate and into the compound.
4 Having resolved the situation, the guard returns to the gatehouse and closes the gate, not realizing there is an enemy agent now on the inside.

A variation involves one of the *shinobi* chasing away a false thief or losing a false fight, then creating a bond with the guard so that they offer the agent shelter inside the compound. This will enable the *shinobi* to identify and possibly unlock any entrance points in readiness for a later infiltration.

ABOVE: A *shinobi* uses a decoy to distract a guard and gain access to a protected gate.

Lesson 34

THE BLOWPIPE TEST

If you see a target seemingly sleeping in a room you wish to enter, you can use a blowpipe to check whether or not they really are asleep. Charge a blowpipe with fine powder, then blow the powder toward the target through an opening above the door

ABOVE: **The blowpipe test in action.**

or any other gap you can find. This should bring about an itching response or similar reaction from a person who is only pretending to be asleep.

Lesson 35

BLOWPIPE ILLUMINATION

Blowpipes can also be used to light up a room briefly. Before the mission, prepare darts packed with a small amount of gunpowder around the spine and a short fuse attached. When you wish to illuminate a dark room, carefully light one of these darts, load it into a blowpipe and blow it into the room. (Make sure you breathe in before you put the pipe to your mouth, to avoid choking on a mouthful of smoke.) When the fuse lights the gunpowder there will be a quick flash giving the infiltrator a "snapshot" of the room.

ABOVE: A small dart with gunpowder attached lights up a room.

Lesson 36

TWO-PERSON ILLUMINATION

The problem with illuminating a dark room is you do not know what you will find in there. You may be met with the vision of a sleeping enemy or a spear thrust to the body. To counter this, *shinobi* have developed a two-pronged observation skill. One *shinobi* will place a light in or near a room while keeping their body back to avoid any attacks; and the other one will look into the room from the opposite side so that their form is hidden but they can still observe the room. This way both *shinobi* will be out of reach from any guards lying in wait and, if there is a trap set, the agents can flee instantly.

ABOVE: A *shinobi* lights a room from one side to divert attention while a second agent observes from the opposite side.

Shinobi skill: The agent lighting the room should do so with their body away from the likely direction of a spear thrust and the other *shinobi* should remain hidden but attentive.

Lesson 37

FIRE ON THE END OF A ROD

A solo *shinobi* can minimize the risk of surprise attack when lighting a room by using a thin bamboo pole with a small amount of torch material at the end. Find a place where you can see into the room and also allow the light to enter, then light the torch end of the pole and push it into the room. This skill was devised for use in Japanese houses, which often have an open, carved section called a *ranma* at the top of the wall, an ideal vantage point.

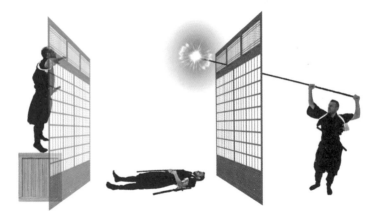

ABOVE: The *shinobi* with the light on a stick is too far away to be attacked.

Lesson 38

PRETENDING TO BE AN ANIMAL TO FIND ENEMY SLEEPING QUARTERS

Even if an infiltrator knows the general layout of an enemy compound, chances are they still will not know exactly where the master of the house sleeps. One way they can find this out is to make the sound of an animal, such as a stray dog barking or a cat yowling, repeatedly throughout the night. Eventually (they hope) the master will wake up, strike a light, open a window shutter or sliding door and shout at the animal or try to chase it away. Then the *shinobi* will know where the target is and can proceed to make the kill.

ABOVE: Barking like a dog can draw out an enemy.

Shinobi **skill:** Fujibayashi-sensei records this skill in the *Bansenshūkai*, but he also advises against using it. Instead, he recommends placing a *kunoichi*, or undercover housemaid, in the target house to relay the correct location to the *shinobi*.

Lesson 39

HIDING THE FACE BEHIND THE SLEEVE

This skill is one of the most important pieces of evidence we have for *shinobi* not wearing the "ninja mask" with which they are often associated. When happening upon a guard, *shinobi* train themselves to be completely still, to "become like stone", and also to hide their paleness of their face behind a sleeve so that it does not catch the light, be it starlight, moonlight or torchlight. By doing this they can evade detection. (See lesson 143 for the mystical aspect of this skill.)

ABOVE: A *shinobi* hides his face to evade detection.

Lesson 40

HOLDING A FALSE CONVERSATION

Imagine it is the darkest part of the night, the sleeping void when the world is at rest. You are inside the labyrinth of an enemy house, but you sense that a guard has become suspicious and is trying to track you down. The guard cannot see you, but they can hear you. Turn this to your advantage by staging a false conversation with an imaginary second *shinobi*. Say something like, "Let's leave here and move to the outhouses" or "I think someone's awake, let's head for the gate." The idea is to misdirect the guard and escape by going in another direction.

Shinobi **skill:** In this situation master *shinobi* display their iron will and phenomenal nerve. Having sent the guard on a false trail, they do not escape but instead push on, deeper into the house, in search of their target.

ABOVE: A *shinobi* holds a false conversation in order to misdirect a suspicious guard.

Lesson 41

SAWING THROUGH A WALL

Shinobi writers often discuss the practice of sawing through walls. Bear in mind that they are not referring to stone or brick walls, but to those of a wattle-and-daub construction consisting of a wooden framework, which holds a lattice of thin strips of wood or bamboo covered with layers of clay and finally a wash of paint. *Shinobi* would work

ABOVE: A *shinobi* uses a saw to cut a hole through a wall.

on the outer part of the wall, breaking away the clay until they exposed the latticework. Then they would saw through the latticework and the clay on the other side until they had made a hole large enough to crawl through. *Shinobi* may also have cut through plain wooden walls.

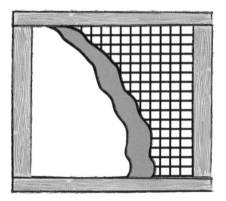

LEFT: A classic Japanese wall construction with a wooden framework and a plaster and paint finish.

Lesson 42

BREAKING IN THROUGH A SLIDING WOODEN DOOR

ABOVE: Working out the exact centre point of a door with a string.

Japanese houses have three main forms of sliding door: the very famous *shōji* (障子), a thin, paper sliding door, which forms main areas; the *fusuma* (襖), which is a thicker paper sliding door that divides rooms into sections; and also the *amado* (雨戸), wooden doors found on the exterior, with a vertical bolt that fits into a hole in the threshold. When the *amado* are closed they create a form of wooden shield around the main body of the house. To get through a bolted *amado* door, press very lightly on the door to assess whether the bolt is located in the centre or at the edge. If the bolt seems to be in the centre, the next task is to find the exact centre. Measure the width of the door with string, then fold the string in half and extend that half measure from the edge of the door to the centre. Then use a U-shaped drill to cut out a small circle in the centre of the door so that you can reach in and lift up the bolt.

ABOVE: The type of drill described in the *Bansenshūkai* and used to cut out small holes.

Lesson 43

INFILTRATING IN DISGUISE, NOT IN STEALTH

"When most people think of infiltrating, they imagine crossing over a moat or climbing up a wall, but these are exceptional measures that shinobi *should take only in an emergency."*

Iga and Kōka Ninja Skills, Chikamatsu Shigenori, 18th century

In this chapter we have focused on infiltration by stealth, but there are other ways to gain access to an enemy stronghold. Disguising yourself as someone who is meant to be in the target area is one such method. This is a common theme in *shinobi* teachings and requires us to widen our understanding of the term infiltration. The fundamental aim of the *shinobi* is not to be seen, but this includes not being seen as a threat.

***Shinobi* skill:** Avoid attracting the wrong type of attention: learn to be the grey man.

ABOVE: A *shinobi* disguised as the servant to a samurai in order to infiltrate an enemy stronghold.

Climbing
Skills

Lesson 44

USING A GRAPPLING HOOK TO CLIMB OVER A WALL

ABOVE: The grappling hook is a key part of the *shinobi* tool kit.

The classic *shinobi* image is of a shadowy figure climbing over a wall and, as this lesson indicates, there is a high degree of truth to that. While climbing higher walls requires a ladder, low walls can be scaled using only a grapple tied to a short rope. The grapple can be flat, raked or have multi-directional prongs and some types are collapsible to make them easier to carry. Grapples work particularly well for hooking over the kind of Japanese house wall that has a small tile roof giving it a lip, or over a wooden palisade around a military camp.

ABOVE: A selection of *shinobi* grappling hooks.

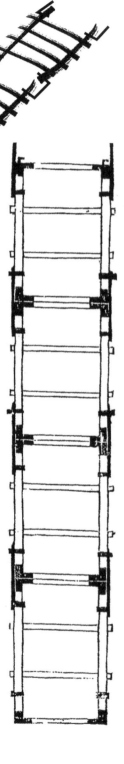

Lesson 45

THE JOINTED LADDER

As its name suggests, this type of ladder can be folded or broken up into sections, which fit together or fold out and are locked in place by a latch system. Fujibayashi-sensei disapproves of the jointed ladder; he believes that all ninja tools should be lightweight and that the jointed ladder is too cumbersome.

RIGHT: A jointed ladder as shown in the *Gunpō Jiyōshū* manual written by the samurai Ogasawara Saku'un Katsuzo in *c*.1612.

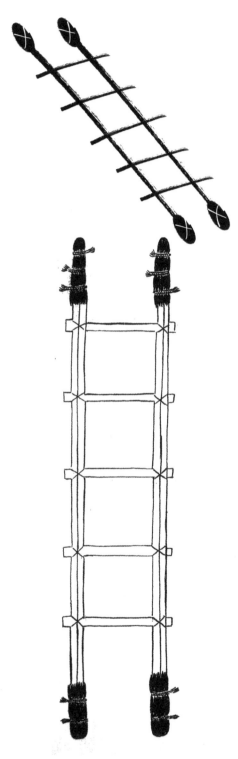

Lesson 46

THE TIED LADDER

The tied ladder consists of two long bamboo poles to form the rails (the two sides of the ladder), with shorter sections of bamboo to form the rungs. Having stealthily measured the height of the wall you intend to climb, return to base camp to source bamboo of the correct length and cut the parts needed for the ladder. These parts can either be assembled in advance, which tends to produce a sturdier construction, or in situ if it would not be practical to carry the preassembled ladder all the way from the base camp. You can wrap straw or soft cloth around the ends of the rails to help keep your efforts as quiet as possible. As well as the bamboo, the only other tools and materials you will need are a saw or a knife, some strong cord and some straw or cloth.

LEFT: A tied ladder, as shown in the *Bansenshūkai*.

Lesson 47

THE FLYING LADDER

The flying ladder consists of a single rail with rungs attached to the rail at the centre of each rung and pads at each end of the rail for soundproofing. The rail is strengthened by gluing and binding strips of bamboo around a central wooden shaft. This is a relatively lengthy process, meaning that the ladder really needs to be made in advance. The flying ladder can be used to scale walls in the normal fashion but also, like other rigid ladders, it can be placed across roofs to enable you to move from one roof to another. Just make sure that the rungs find a good purchase.

Lesson 48

THE CLOUD LADDER

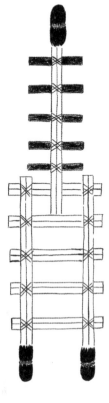

Many ladders found in *shinobi* manuals are smaller versions of Chinese military ladders. This is the case with the cloud ladder, which is a combination of the tied ladder and the flying ladder (see lessons 46 and 47). Although shorter than the Chinese version, the *shinobi* cloud ladder enables soldiers to climb the highest fortress walls or get a good vantage over a distant location. The *shinobi* squad will carry a flying ladder and a tied ladder to the site of infiltration and then join them together in situ to create a cloud ladder.

RIGHT: A cloud ladder as shown in the *Bansenshūkai*.

Lesson 49

THE ROLLED LADDER

The rolled ladder is a relatively short ladder consisting of a single length of rope that folds over in the middle to form two rails. Then bamboo rungs are attached to the rope rails. To measure the correct length of the ladder, hold your arms up directly above your head. The length should be the distance from the ground to your wrist. (You will see why this is the case in the following lesson.) This ladder can be rolled and lashed up and carried to the target area or can be assembled on site.

ABOVE: A rolled ladder as shown in the *Bansenshūkai*.

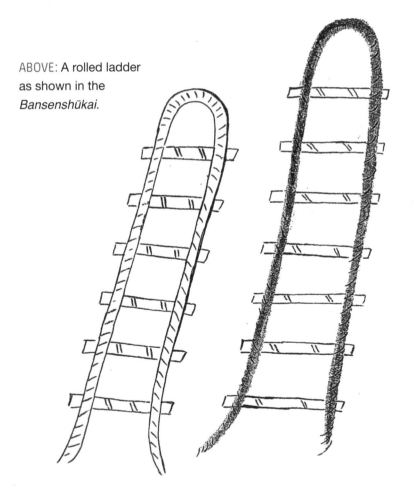

Lesson 50

USING TWO ROLLED LADDERS IN COMBINATION

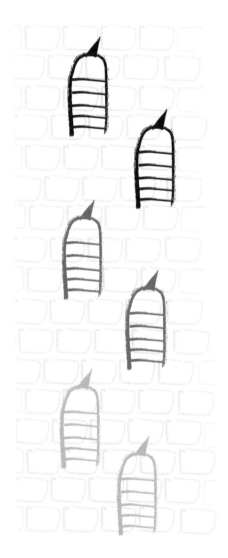

A single *shinobi* can use a pair of rolled ladders to scale a wall much higher than either ladder. First reach as high as possible and jab a spike into the wall, then hook the looped end of one of the ladders onto the spike. Climb the ladder, then reach up again and jab the second spike into the wall, either directly above you or above and to the right side. Hook the second ladder on and move your body weight onto it. Next remove the first ladder and spike and move to the top of the second ladder. Again reach as high as possible and insert the first spike, this time to the left, and hook on the first ladder. Do this repeatedly until you reach the top of the wall.

Shinobi **skill:** The base walls of Japanese castles are made of large rocks wedged together, meaning that you can fit your spikes into the cracks between blocks.

ABOVE: A single *shinobi* can use a pair of rolled ladders to climb up the wall.

Lesson 51

THE SPIKED LADDER

The spiked ladder is similar to the rolled ladder except that it has spikes attached to its rope rails. Start by attaching the lower spikes into the cracks then, rung by rung, ascend the ladder anchoring the higher spikes as you go. When you have attached all the spikes, climb back down the ladder and unhook the lower spikes, leaving just a few anchor points at the top. Then pull the bottom of the ladder up as far as possible, and secure the lower parts again, this time higher than before. When they are secure, you can unhook the top parts and move upwards. The whole process is relatively lengthy and mimics the motion of a slowly crawling caterpillar, which repeatedly pulls up its back end to climb a wall.

Shinobi **skill:** As the profile of the castle wall shows (lesson 74), Japanese fortifications are sloped not vertical making it easier for the *shinobi* to lean backwards and work each spike.

Lesson 52

THE LARGE HOOK

This is a larger-than-normal hook and it folds in half. When folded out it can be pinned into position. The *Bansenshūkai* gives dimensions for the tool, but does not describe how it should be used. However, we can hypothesize that it serves as a robust climbing aid to enable a *shinobi* squad to climb a wall relatively quickly. Most likely a single *shinobi* will scale a wall using one of the slower methods, such as a pair of rolled ladders or a spiked ladder. Having reached the top, the lead *shinobi* anchors the large hook in place and attaches a long rope to it. This allows the rest of the team to climb up the rope, which can, of course, also be used for a quick escape.

Escape and Hiding Skills

Lesson 53

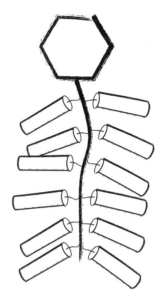

THE FIRECRACKER ESCAPE

When preparing to infiltrate a military compound, set up a series of firecrackers in foliage near to your planned exit point with a fuse ready to light. If you are detected and need to flee to your exit point, you or a second agent standing by can light the fuse using embers carried in a tool called a *dōnohi*. This sets off the firecrackers, which replicate the sound and flashes of musket fire, causing the pursuing enemy to take cover from the "ghost shooters" while they structure their defence and allowing you to make your escape.

Shinobi **skill:** Ensure that you charge each firecracker with an amount of gunpowder similar to that used in a musket shot.

Lesson 54

QUAIL-HIDING

Quail-hiding is named after the Japanese quail (*Coturnix japonica*), a rotund bird known as the *uzura* in its native land. When you are in a tight spot, get down on the ground and curl up as tightly as possible. Stay as still as you can and "as quiet as frost on the ground" while chanting the *ongyō* spell of hiding (see lesson 143).

According to Fujibayashi-sensei, the five advantages of quail-hiding are:

- It hides the white of your face and other exposed skin.
- By facing down, your energy corresponds to the male element of *yō*.

81

- The enemy will not be able to see your breath (if it is cold enough to condense).
- It makes you smaller and stops you from looking like a person.
- It prevents you from looking at the enemy and getting frightened.

Shinobi **skill:** Directions have male or female (*yō* or *in*) associations. The downward direction aligns with the male *yō* element, so it is considered beneficial for *shinobi* (who are predominantly male) to face down. However, this advantage does not apply to female *shinobi*.

Lesson 55

THE RACCOON-DOG RETREAT

When you have a pursuer close on your tail, one tactic that can be effective is to suddenly come to a halt and assume a crouching position like a raccoon dog. Not having time to stop, your pursuer will fall over you, allowing you to draw your sword and kill him.

However, be aware that this skill can be countered by someone who chases from one side or the other rather than directly behind you. That way you cannot come to a halt and knock them off balance, you have to keep running. An experienced pursuer chasing you with a spear will stay on your right; if chasing with a sword, they will stay on your left (see lesson 111).

Lesson 56

RACCOON-DOG HIDING

Raccoon-dog hiding involves climbing a large tree and hiding at a great height within the foliage. While this sounds simple, it takes a certain degree of athleticism to reach the lower branches of a large tree and "spider-climb" to the higher parts.

Shinobi **skill:** Before using this skill make absolutely sure no one can see what you are doing. If your pursuers see you climbing into a tree they will simply surround it and kill you at their leisure. This skill is all about getting yourself high off the ground and in a position where the enemy will not think to look.

ABOVE: A *shinobi* must make sure they have not been spotted before they climb a tree with the intention of concealing themself within it.

Lesson 57

THE CALTROP RETREAT

Shinobi are infamous for their use of caltrops, which are small metal spikes. Often caltrops are used to hinder your pursuers when you are escaping after an infiltration mission, but they can also be positioned along the inside of the walls of your own compound to defend against enemy *shinobi*. Issui-sensei tells us that this is done only when you are expecting an enemy infiltration.

There are three main ways to use caltrops when retreating:

- Caltrop trains – stretch out multiple caltrops on a cord.
- Scattered caltrops – scatter caltrops behind you as you make your escape.
- Pre-positioned caltrops – prepare your escape by putting caltrops in certain positions before a mission.

   Shinobi **skill:** Be fully aware of the huge number of caltrops you will need. *Shinobi* use caltrops on an industrial scale!

RIGHT: A caltrop train; caltrops are tied to a rope and dragged behind a *shinobi*.

Lesson 58

WALKING THROUGH CALTROPS

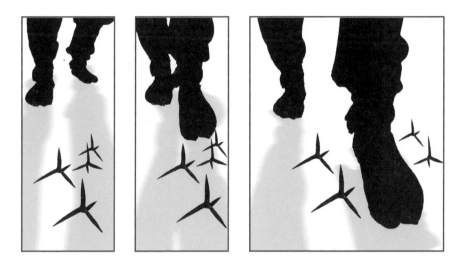

ABOVE: Keeping their feet flat to the ground, the *shinobi* slides past the caltrops, pushing them out of the way with the tips of their toes.

When you are walking through an area where you know or suspect there are caltrops, move your feet in a style of long shuffle called *suriashi*. The idea is to slide your feet without lifting them off the ground so that you push the caltrops out of the way rather than stepping on them.

Alternatively, Issui-sensei teaches us either to use a common house brush to sweep the caltrops away or to crawl along the ground swiping at them horizontally with a spear.

***Shinobi* skill:** Remember that caltrops can be made of bamboo or iron and come in different shapes and designs.

Night Attack Skills

Lesson 59

TYPES OF NIGHT ATTACK

There are various types of night attack, from large-scale battles at night (*yoikusa*) down to raids by small bands of troops (*yogomi*). However, the general term for a night attack is *youchi* – made up of 夜 ("night") and 討 ("attack"). In a standard night attack a relatively large group of soldiers will move out under cover of darkness and invade an enemy camp. The invasion will often be timed to coincide with a fire attack within the camp performed by *shinobi* who have managed to enter in advance.

Some night attacks are carried out exclusively in a *shinobi* manner, these are called *shinobi-youchi*. These attacks tend to involve a group of *shinobi* raiding an enemy camp or household to inflict a specific kind of physical damage – to burn the stores, for example. The main point to understand here is that *shinobi* night raids (*shinobi-youchi*) differ from *shinobi* infiltration missions (*shinobi-iru*). While both require stealth, night raids are sudden strikes at the enemy that they will know about as soon as they happen, whereas the object of an infiltration mission is to steal in silently and discreetly to achieve an objective that the enemy will not necessarily discover until later.

SHINOBI-
IRU

SHINOBI-
YOUCHI

Lesson 60

WHAT TO WEAR AND CARRY ON A NIGHT ATTACK

This lesson refers to the standard night attack described in the previous lesson, in which a large number of conventional troops will attempt to invade an enemy camp – most likely in conjunction with an internal fire attack performed by dedicated *shinobi*. For such an attack, it is good for the members of the attacking party to wear basic armour but without a back banner. They will also wear a *haori* jacket and an identification marker. Shorter weapons such as spears without hooks, swords or short bows are better than polearms and long bows, which can catch in foliage or narrow places. For the same reason, it is advisable for soldiers not to wear high-crested helmets.

Lesson 61

TAGGING HEADS

Just like any other type of Japanese soldier, *shinobi* will want to capture the heads of the enemies they kill to demonstrate their individual prowess. However, this poses particular problems during a night raid, which must be focused and well coordinated. If warriors keep stopping to remove the heads of slain enemies, they will lose momentum. To address this difficulty, soldiers take wooden tags with their names on them to either attach or stab into the enemy. If they are victorious then the allies can read the tags and identify who killed whom. If they do not succeed in taking the area, then the enemy will read the tags instead. In either case records should be kept.

Lesson 62

WITHDRAWING ON A SIGNAL

A night raid is a rapid strike requiring coordination and adroitness. Everyone involved needs to know exactly when and how to retreat. The raid commander will order a signal to be given when he deems that the raid has been successful or that the time has come for the troops to withdraw. The signal should be a sound because a flag will not be visible in the darkness and a fire signal will not stand out from any other burning that is around. When they hear the signal, troops should disengage from combat and follow the prearranged exit strategy.

Lesson 63

SWEEPING AND STABBING WITH A SPEAR

When an attack squad is moving in darkness, all members should gently sweep from side to side with their spear. If they feel it touch something, they should draw the spear back and then thrust to stab whatever the spear has touched. Often it will just be a tree, but occasionally it will be an enemy lying in wait. While hooked spears are good for ensnaring and tripping an enemy, they are likely to become annoying on a night raid when they keep catching on unseen obstacles. A straight spear will be much better.

Lesson 64

COORDINATED HAND-GRENADE ATTACKS

Fires and explosions play a vital role in night attacks. In this lesson we will focus on hand grenades. Traditional Japanese hand grenades comprise two hollow clay hemispheres filled with gunpowder (and sometimes shrapnel) and then bound into a sphere using layers of paper. They may sometimes have rope attached to propel them further. The aim is for a *shinobi* squad to creep up as close as possible to the enemy and, on command, launch a coordinated grenade attack. This will throw the enemy into disarray and enable allied troops to take them down with ease.

ABOVE: A *shinobi* squad moves in fast and deploys clay hand grenades in a coordinated attack.

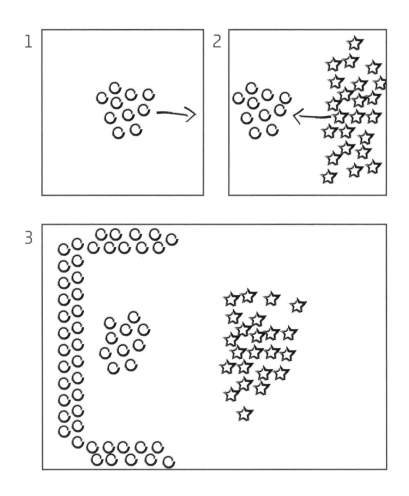

Lesson 65

SENDING IN A BAIT TEAM

A worthy enemy will be prepared for night attacks and have troops ready to counterattack. One way to overcome these is to send in a team as bait to tempt the enemy into sending out its counter squad. On a given signal the bait group will retreat to a pre-planned position where an ambush lies in wait. The enemy's counter squad will follow the bait team and be slaughtered by the ambush. This will discourage the enemy from sending out any more men, and they will be pinned inside their battle camp.

Lesson 66

OVERT AND COVERT SIGNALS

Signals may be either overt or covert, depending on the situation. If it is obvious the enemy knows your force is in position, there is no need to disguise your signals. You just have to make sure that the enemy cannot understand them. Like Morse code, the sounds are meaningless unless you know how to decipher them. Each side will create its own system of signals, ranging from the simple to the complex.

Conversely, if hidden operatives are working in secret near the enemy, they may use everyday sounds that will not raise suspicion, such as a town or temple bell, as prearranged signals to coordinate their moves.

***Shinobi* skill:** Musical instruments such as the Japanese flute, conch shells, drums and cymbals can be used to deliver either overt or covert signals. If you are in a battle camp and you hear, for example, enemy conch shells or drums sounding out, you will know they are signals but you will not understand their meaning. On the other hand, a spy who is operating undercover in an enemy settlement can play a tune without the enemy suspecting that it is, in fact, a signal.

Defensive Skills

Lesson 67

IDENTIFICATION MARKINGS

Samurai identify themselves in two ways: firstly, they have to display their prowess and personal identity as a warrior; secondly, they have to exhibit army or division markers. Personal identification is done through helmet crests, spear scabbards, banners, flags, coloured armour, etc. Some soldiers attach a piece of cloth to the rear of the helmet or on the sleeve, or even tie cloth directly on an arm or leg. Furthermore, Issui-sensei tells us that the sword cord (*sageo*) can be used as a hidden marker, with members of a team all wearing cords of the same colour. A warrior needs to both belong to a unit and stand out.

Shinobi **skill:** The skills in this chapter are those used to defend against *shinobi* infiltration. *Shinobi* need to understand these skills and find ways to counter them. For example, you must discover the correct identification markers, passwords and any form of secret signals before you infiltrate an enemy force. Otherwise, you will be quickly found out.

Lesson 68

PASSWORDS AND SIGNS

Following on from the previous lesson, passwords are divided between two separate orders:

1. AIKOTOBA (相詞) – PASSWORDS

Samurai passwords come in two parts, with each part consisting of a word that links to the other. For example, a guard might say "moon" to which the correct response of a soldier wishing to enter might be "sun". Other simple pairings of this nature include "hill" / "valley" or "positive" / "negative". However, the association may be more subtle, such as a connection to a poem or a legend, e.g. "Arthur" / "Excalibur", "Marcus Aurelius" / "Meditations" or "Homer" / "Iliad". The idea is to make them easy to remember once they have been revealed, but hard to work out straightaway.

2. TACHISUGURI ISUGURI (立ちすぐり居すぐり) – GESTURES OF IDENTIFICATION

Certain movements can act in a similar way to passwords. When suspecting that enemy *shinobi* have infiltrated the group, a troop leader may give a command word upon which everyone drops to a crouch. Any infiltrators will not know this and so will be left standing and identifiable.

TACHISUGURT ISUGURI　立ちすぐり居すぐり

AIJIRUSHI　相印

AIKOTOBA　相詞

Lesson 69

WIFE AND CHILD HOSTAGES

The world of the samurai was founded on loyalty pledged to a lord, but loyalties could shift. Or an apparently trustworthy warrior might turn out to be an enemy *shinobi*. Recognizing these facts of life, a lord had certain strategies to guarantee the loyalty of his retainers. For example, when giving an oath of allegiance samurai would often have to surrender their family as hostages to the clan. The family lived in

relative comfort according to its station within a castle complex, city or town, but was always under the threat of death if the retainer changed his loyalty or revealed himself to be an enemy agent.

To counter this practice, a *shinobi* infiltrator would deliver a fake wife and children so that when he double-crossed the enemy lord, the fate of the woman and children was of no consequence to him.

Did the wife and children know they were doomed, or were they also agents who had an escape plan? It is hard to say, but what is clear is that the lives of women and children would sometimes have been used up in the schemes of the *shinobi*, lending truth to Issui-sensei's warning that the path of the *shinobi* is *horrifying*.

Lesson 70

RAKED SAND TRENCHES

Around the perimeter of a battle camp are earthen-walled guard stations next to which fires burn all night, projecting an arc of light out into the darkness where the *shinobi* lie in wait. The only dark areas on the perimeter are between the guard stations, and it is these gaps that the *shinobi* will target. To counter this apparent weakness, the defenders dig shallow but wide trenches and fill them with sand, which is raked like that in a Zen garden. The trenches are shallow enough that an infiltrator can walk across them, but too wide to jump over. This means that any infiltrator will leave footprints in the sand, so when night patrols see them they can raise the alarm and cry, "Intruder, intruder!"

ABOVE: Two guards at a watch fire with sand trenches at either side. Many of these will come together to form a perimeter.

Lesson 71

USING TORCHES TO SEE OVER WALLS

Shinobi take refuge in the darkness at the base of a moat or ditch outside of the walls of a fort, castle or compound. To shed light on these dark places, defenders lower torches attached to ropes over the wall. Viewed from a distance

an onlooker would see bright specks of light being lowered and raised from a castle battlements to the dark areas below.

LEFT: A *shinobi* hides in the shadows as a guard searches for intruders in the darkness.

Lesson 72

ABOVE: Diagram of a traditional medieval Japanese loin cloth.

SHINOBI-PROOF UNDERWEAR

In the dark of night, a counter-attack team waits behind the camp gate, ready to move out into the night and engage with the besieging enemy. Such a massive amount of movement in the dark gives *shinobi* a chance to infiltrate. They can do this either by stealing in through the gate as the attack squad moves out, or by pretending to be a member of the returning attack group. Remember, some of the attack group will have been killed in the engagement, so there will be space for an agent to mingle. Also the group will need to come back in quickly, so there may not be time for a password protocol. However, be aware that the enemy may have other ways to detect infiltrators.

One such method used in old Japan would be to issue each member of an attack team with undergarments of the same colour and texture, so that when they undressed on the inside of the camp, anyone wearing a garment of the wrong colour or texture would be identified immediately.

Lesson 73

STAMPED PASSES

Another way to control access to a camp during the sending and retrieving of a night squad is to use tags or passes. These are sections of paper, cloth or bamboo, etc. that have an official stamp on them. The number of passes issued corresponds exactly to the number of soldiers in the squad (plus one control pass to be kept at the gate) and the same passes are never used for more than one mission. This makes it difficult for a *shinobi* to get hold of one.

As the troops come back through the gate they return the stamped pass to the guard who compares it to the control pass to make sure it is correct. The guard may also check that they give the correct password and any accompanying gestures and that that they are wearing the correct identification marks and the right colour underwear.

To summarize, these are the five ways to detect *shinobi* (as given in the *Bansenshūkai*):

- stamped passes
- passwords
- gestures when giving passwords
- identification marks
- underwear

Lesson 74

OBSERVING CASTLE AND FORT DEFENCES

Japanese forts typically make use of a number of ingenious defence mechanisms. These include: retractable drawbridges, collapsible walls, fake walls and trapping

zones, stone-dropping ports (see illustration opposite), sally ports, spikes of various types (see lesson 75), and many other ways to deceive and repel an enemy. The task of the *shinobi* before or during a siege is to discover the location and function of all the defences so that a commander can assault the most vulnerable parts of the fortress. Mapping out castles and infiltrating at night to discover the defensive layout is an essential aspect of this work.

LEFT: Cross-section of a stone dropping port. The external view can be seen at the bottom of the opposite page.

Lesson 75

SPIKES

Different types of spiked defence are positioned in the areas surrounding a castle.

NAIL BOARDS

Nails are hammered through wooden boards, which are then laid upon the ground.

ABOVE: Spiked nail boards are left on the ground to stop troops and enemy *shinobi*.

STAKE CLUSTERS

Stakes are driven into the ground in groups of five and hidden using thick foliage and bushes woven in between them.

PITFALLS

Pits are dug 2 metres (6–7 feet) deep and sharpened spikes placed inside. The pits are covered with a weave of bamboo, soil and foliage, which disguises them but does not stop people falling through.

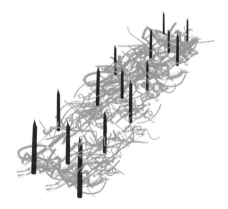

ABOVE: Thick foliage conceals spikes designed to stop the enemy.

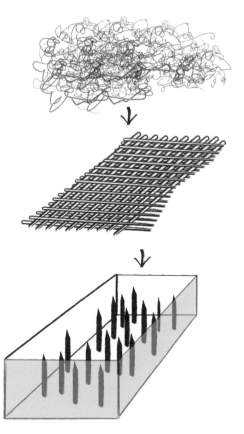

ABOVE RIGHT: The presence of pitfall traps will make any enemies cautious of moving forward at speed.

Lesson 76

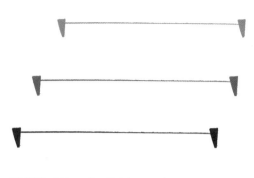

TRIP WIRES

Trip wires vary in scale, from simple cords positioned around private houses, all the way up to complex networks of ropes around fortifications or even in rivers. These can be either hidden or in plain

ABOVE: Trip-wire fields can be very intricate and cover large areas.

view. Concealed trip wires are designed to surprise an enemy, whereas visible ones, often particularly extensive and complex, are designed to deter the enemy from taking that route. Intricate rope systems may contain special pathways for defending troops to move through.

Lesson 77

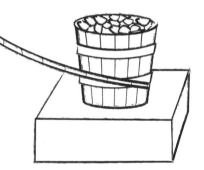

THE DOOR TRAP

There are multiple variations on the idea of a booby trap rigged to a door to catch out an infiltrator entering a room. In the *Bansenshūkai* Fujibayashi-sensei describes a rope attached to a sliding door so that when the door opens the rope pulls over a bucket laden with pebbles,

ABOVE: A bucket of pebbles tied to a door makes an effective alarm.

creating a scattering fuss. Issui-sensei gives us two versions: in the *Heika Jōdan* he uses a balanced Japanese fan so that when the door opens the fan wakes the sleeper inside the room; and in the *Shōninki* he recommends tying a cord between a sliding door and a samurai's topknot so that the tug on the samurai's hair when the door opens wakes him up.

Communication Skills

Lesson 78

THE SUBSTITUTION CIPHER

A substitution cipher is a fixed code system in which each letter is replaced by another letter or symbol, e.g. A = 1, B = 2, etc. By today's standards this is extremely simple, but on the battlefronts of old Japan, where time was of the essence, such a system was adequate. By the time the code had been broken, the situation would most likely have moved on and there would be a new set of messages using a new cipher. And as the following lessons show, there are various strategies to make coded messages harder to decipher.

Shinobi **skill:** Study the subject of cryptography and understand the differences between ciphers and codes and their sub-labels.

A	B	C	D	E	F	G	H	I	J	K	L	M	N	O	P	Q	R	S	T	U	V	W	X	Y	Z
+	@	¡	§	Æ	≈	··	∫	~"	Δ	«	≥≤	Œ	∂	∧	Π	Ұ	¶	⊠	⊡	∶	ℭ	∞	≠	太	✝

Lesson 79

CUTTING A SECRET NOTE INTO SECTIONS

One way to make a coded letter harder to crack is to cut it up into sections and have different messengers deliver each section. Even if the enemy manage to intercept one section and decode it they still will not understand what the whole message is about, and the intended recipient will know that an interception has taken place. For added security, cut the coded letter along the centre of the ideograms so that the sections form complete words only when they are all put back together at the destination.

Lesson 80

ARROW LETTERS

To communicate with a secret agent inside a fortress, attach a message to a headless arrow and fire it over the wall at a prearranged time and location. Arrow letters may also be used to send open messages to an enemy leader or to contact a troop commander who is manning a certain section of a defensive wall with an offer of payment for defection or assistance in an infiltration.

Shinobi **skill:** Another devious use of the arrow letter is to send false reports into a castle to spread discord and confusion among the enemy forces.

RIGHT: This image from the *Bansenshūkai* (modified for clarity) is without explanation or reference in the original manual. However, it appears to be an arrow letter.

Lesson 81

FLAG SIGNALS FOR THE DAYTIME

Shinobi performing reconnaissance ahead of an army do not always need to hide themselves from the enemy, as the enemy will often be well aware that an army is on the move in their lands. Therefore, flags can be used to signal backwards and forwards between the *shinobi* and the main body of the army. Different colour flags moved in different ways convey different messages. What the army commander most commonly wants to know is whether it is safe to proceed in a certain direction.

***Shinobi* skill:** Flags can also be used for individual *shinobi* to communicate with each other when away from the army.

ABOVE: Flags can provide an effective means of two-way communication between a *shinobi* scout and a following army.

113

Lesson 82

FIRE SIGNALS FOR THE NIGHT TIME

During night-time reconnaissance *shinobi* use fire to signal back to the army commander. Chikamatsu-sensei notes that the way *shinobi* locate a fire in relation to a tree (either in front of the tree or behind it from the vantage point of the allied troops) can be used to convey different meanings. This is just one example of the diversity and complexity of fire signals. They range from candles and torches all the way to large bonfires and rockets fired from tall towers. Sometimes *shinobi* burn down buildings or even whole towns for the purpose of signalling.

Shinobi **skill:** The use of fire as a signal is one of the largest areas of study for a student of *shinobi no jutsu*. This lesson is just to emphasize to you what an important subject this is.

ABOVE: A *shinobi* holding a basic torch. Torches such as this were often designed to be waterproof.

Lesson 83

CONCH SHELL SIGNAL

Used extensively by the Yamabushi, a group of Japanese mountain-dwelling hermits, conch shells can be converted into horn trumpets with a mouthpiece. The conch can make a wide variety of sounds through different lengths and strengths of blowing, trilling and dampening, all of which can be codified to convey different messages. The *shinobi* will create their own system of conch shell signals.

Shinobi **skill:** Systems such as Morse code and semaphore flags are good examples of how complex messages can be built up from small elements. Any signalling system needs to include special codes that denote the start and end of a message and alert the receiver when an error has been made.

Aquatic
Skills

Lesson 84

THE WAY OF WATER

Shinobi should have an excellent understanding of water and the way it flows, because water is needed to sustain an army and it can help or hinder a force in its movements. This lesson gives an overview of some of the key concepts relating to rivers.

A river can flow in any direction, north, south, east or west, but it must start from higher ground and move to a lower level, from its source on a hill- or mountainside down to the sea or other large body of water. Some rivers end up underground. Rivers have three main sections: the upper course, the middle course and the lower course. At its source even the mightiest river may be no more than an amalgamation of small trickling streams. Along the way it may take in smaller tributaries, or it may itself flow into a larger river. It may meander to such an extent that it creates an oxbow lake, which is a small body of water that has been cut off from the main river. To either side of the river may be marshes and certain areas that will become floodplains at times of high rainfall. The river will vary in depth; it will have rapids where the riverbed is particularly steep; it will have riffles, which are shallow fast areas; there will be pools where water collects and slows down and it will also have runs, which are sections of steady flow. At the end of the river is the mouth

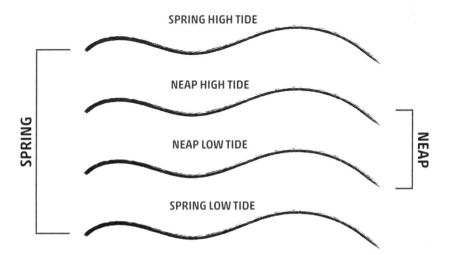

ABOVE: Diagram showing the different levels of spring and neap tides.

where sediment is deposited and a series of small land masses may form in a delta, or it may form an estuary, where the river meets the sea and freshwater and seawater intermingle. (See lesson 132 for a discussion of tides.)

***Shinobi* skill:** One of the *shinobi's* responsibilities is to find a suitable place for an army to camp. This requires knowledge of the way of water, so that you do not, for example, site a camp on a floodplain just before the start of the rainy season or in a valley during torrential rain. A student of *shinobi* arts must always consider the subjects of geography and meteorology from the point of view of a military commander.

Lesson 85

CROSSING A MARSH

Often castles and military camps that border a marsh are less well defended on that side, because it is hard for attacking troops to cross a wetland without getting stuck and becoming an easy target for projectile weapons. Therefore, commanders do not feel they need to position many guards there. However, *shinobi* have various ways to cross a marsh and so they may choose to infiltrate from that direction.

Cross marshes by using one of the following techniques:

- two flat wooden boards – stand on one while pushing the other forward
- marsh shoes – made like snow shoes, or as larger flat boards attached to the feet
- two square lattices made of woven bamboo to lie or stand on
- large mats to lie or stand on

Lesson 86

CROSSING A RIVER USING A GOOD SWIMMER

To get troops across a fast-flowing river, first attach a thin cord to the strongest swimmer who then swims across. The other troop members stay on the bank keeping hold of the other end of the cord. It does not matter if the swimmer is pushed downstream, as long as the cord is long enough to allow them to get across. Having reached the other side, the swimmer stands directly opposite the rest of the troop. The troop members securely tie a heavy line to their end of the cord and the advance swimmer pulls it across and attaches it to a tree or other sturdy anchor point. The troop members then pull it tight to create a hand hold and start to cross one by one while keeping hold of the rope at all times.

Lesson 87

THE FLOATING BRIDGE

Shinobi manuals document various methods to cross over water, including one called the floating bridge, certain details of which are unclear. The bridge is formed of two rope supports with split-bamboo rungs and is anchored on either side of a river or moat using heavy-duty iron spikes. What is not clear is its position in relation to the water – whether it should be suspended

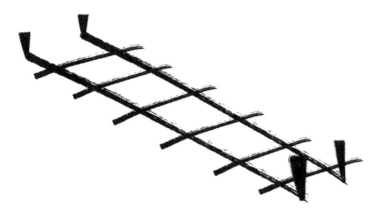

above the water or floating on the surface. It is also open to question whether you should cross over it by crawling or by walking. However, another more robust version uses bamboo poles for the supports and a bamboo lattice to form a deck.

Lesson 88

CROSSING WATER WITHOUT MAKING RIPPLES

When crossing a castle moat, move as slowly as possible to avoid creating ripples on the surface. Even if you are crossing well away from the nearest guard station, ripples can travel a long way and make guards suspicious. Hikone Castle in the Shiga Prefecture has a specific watch tower which houses a guard whose sole responsibility is to look out for ripples in the water below.

"Take a water fowl that has had its wings clipped and put it on a moat. When the enemy's spy approaches, the waterfowl will beat its wings and create a fuss. In this way you will know when the enemy is approaching."

Giyōshū, Ohara Masanori, 1690

Lesson 89

STEPPING IN WATER AND MARSHES

It is hard to walk through shallow water or marshland without making slopping, squelching and sloshing sounds, which draw unwelcome attention to an infiltrator. To counter this the *shinobi* use a step called *nukiashi* (抜足), which means "to draw up the foot" – this stops the foot dragging through the water and reduces the noise you make.

The *nukiashi* technique is as follows:

- Pull up one foot slowly with the toes pointed downwards.
- Slowly and gently withdraw the foot from the water.
- Move forwards.
- Slowly put the foot back into the water, again with the toes pointing downwards (this minimizes the area of the foot breaking the surface of the water, which reduces splashing).
- Take the next step.

Lesson 90

THE FLOATING SEAT

Sometimes mistakenly thought to be a water-walking tool worn on the feet, the much-debated *mizugumo* is in fact a floating water seat made of inflatable leather tubes that are held around the body on a wooden frame. It can be folded away for easy transportation. *Shinobi* use these to move safely across bodies of water or to hide at night in the darkness of the sea or a lake. The name comes either from the *mizugumo* spider, which creates an air bubble to allow it to work underwater, or from the pond skater, which appears to glide on water and may well be the source of the misconception about this tool.

LEFT: The infamous *mizugumo* floating seat of the *Bansenshūkai*.

ABOVE: Examples
of *mizugumo*-like
floats from an Edo-
period image.

Lesson 91

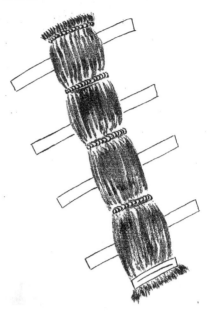

THE CATTAIL RAFT

Taken from old Chinese manuals, the cattail raft is a bundle of cattails (bulrushes) bound tightly together with horizontal bars at intervals. The *shinobi* needs only rope and a knife to construct such a raft when in the field. You can then use it to travel down a river or across a moat.

Lesson 92

THE WAR BOAT

The *shinobi* war boat is a commando-style canoe with a wooden frame and leather waterproofed skin. It can be assembled and disassembled: a version described in the *Bansenshūkai* fits perfectly into a traditional Japanese luggage box. This makes it relatively easy for a *shinobi* team to carry to a launch point from where they will perform their night raid.

Shinobi **skill:** Students of *shinobi* arts should become proficient in aquatic activities such as water craft, kayaking and canoeing – working alone or in teams.

RIGHT: A simplified artist's impression of a war boat.

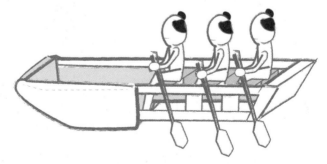

Scouting
Skills

Lesson 93

LONG-DISTANCE SCOUTS

The historical *shinobi* would have been sent out hundreds of miles from their base to scout all over Japan, covering deep valleys, dense, far-stretching forests, wide, gushing rivers and forbidding mountains. Scouting of this nature takes you along dark roads, across snake-infested wilds and involves long periods spent alone, shunning areas of human habitation. These arduous journeys require an extremely high level of proficiency in what would today be termed wilderness survival or bushcraft. From a tactician's point of view, multiple long-distance scouts should be sent out well in advance of any operation. You also need to consider how they can relay their reports back to base for analysis.

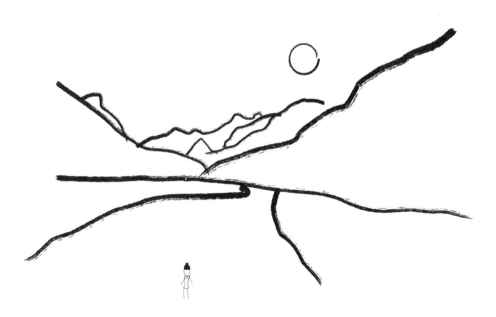

Lesson 94

OUTSIDE LISTENING SCOUTS

The scouting function known as *togiki* is formed from the ideograms 外 ("outside") and 聞 ("listening"). Issui-sensei and Fujibayashi-sensei differ in the way they use the term, although both interpretations can be considered as "listening from the outside". For Issui-sensei, *togiki* means a scout who assumes a disguise to walk among the enemy and pick up information through casual conversation and listening out for rumours. Fujibayashi-sensei uses the term to refer to clandestine commando-scouts who hide around a castle to listen out for intruders.

Lesson 95

SMELLING SCOUTS

"Competent ninja, even if they have accomplished the extraordinary, make no sound, leave no smell and get no fame or honour for their bravery."

Bansenshūkai, Fujibayashi-sensei, 1676

Various military manuals refer to *kagi* (嗅) scouts, including the *Bansenshūkai*, as a kind of "smelling scout" who sniffs out the enemy. One of the meanings of *kagi* is "to smell". There are also frequent references to *shinobi* being used to smell out enemy fuses. A keen nose can pick up human sweat, gunpowder, burning torches, oils and other odours signifying the presence of the enemy close by. This is why it is so important to be downwind or in the lee of the enemy.

Shinobi skill: *Shinobi* can use their nose to identify any foreign bodies moving through a natural landscape.

Lesson 96

LISTENING FROM THE LEEWARD SIDE

Continuing on from lessons 31 and 95, the idea of being in the lee of the enemy is paramount. Not only smells but also sounds carry much better downwind. What's more, any sounds you make will not carry so well upwind.

Shinobi **skill:** Always consider the wind and its direction, but remember that the wind can change or may not be strong enough to have an effect.

Lesson 97

KILLING A SENTRY

Fortifications are surrounded by fire watchmen, listening scouts, smelling scouts, relay teams and light and dark patrols (see lesson 22), all of whom use security measures such as identification marks, passwords and secret movement gestures. To gain entry into a castle, *shinobi* need to overcome these procedures. While they can use scouting skills to witness an exchange of passwords and gestures, sometimes they may kill a sentry in order to get hold of the correct identification marks and to take the place of the guard and enter the castle at the end of the guard's watch. Fujibayashi-sensei warns that killing should be done only for tactical reasons, not out of simple hot-bloodedness.

Shinobi **skill:** When going in for a kill, *shinobi* always approach their target from the leeward side and avoid tangling with branches or foliage and stepping on dry leaves. They may stab their target through the eye with a blade to "switch off the brain".

Lesson 98

INSPECTING ENTRAILS

In siege warfare, one of the core aims of the *shinobi* is to find out what is happening inside the fortification under siege. An important aspect of this is gauging food stocks. They do this indirectly by inspecting the stomach contents of any enemy soldiers left dead outside the main fortification walls. They cut open the stomach and look inside. If it contains rice and vegetables, this means that food levels are still good. However, if the soldier has been eating less desirable things such as leather, tree bark or other improvised foodstuffs, this shows that the castle's stocks have been used up and that the inhabitants are turning to desperate measures. This information can help the commander decide whether or not to continue the siege.

Lesson 99

INFILTRATING AN APPROACHING ARMY

If a lord gets wind that an enemy force is approaching, he can send out his *shinobi* to infiltrate the army while it is en route. The closer the army gets to its target the tighter its security becomes, so *shinobi* should be sent out as early as possible – as soon as the whisper of war is uttered. During periods of peace, warlords tend to reduce the size of their retinue, so they often need to pick up mercenaries, known as *rōnin*, while on the march. This gives a defender the opportunity to place agents in an enemy force weeks or months before the sides meet.

RŌNIN

LEFT: Two different ideogram versions of *rōnin*.

A WORD ON RŌNIN

It is a common misconception that when a samurai lost his lord he had to commit suicide or be cut adrift as a *rōnin*, unable to gain employment with another lord. However, during the warring periods of the samurai age it was not unusual for a samurai to serve different masters over his career. Two terms were created to differentiate between samurai of long and short tenure:

- *fudaimono* – samurai from families who had served for more than one generation
- *tozama* – samurai from families who were yet to serve more than one generation

These two terms were later used to distinguish between those families who had supported the Tokugawa rise to power (which marked the beginning of the Edo period) and those who had not.

It is true that during one brief period in peacetime samurai who became *rōnin* found themselves marooned outside the social system and were barred from serving another master. However, the rules were soon relaxed and *rōnin* could once again become contracted as samurai. This slender slice of time has come to misrepresent *rōnin*, perhaps because of the appeal of the outcast as a story hook for films. In truth, just like in any other walk of life, some *rōnin* prospered and others did not.

Lesson 100

IDENTIFYING LANDING ZONES FOR WATERCRAFT

The samurai are not often associated with sea warfare, but they had a refined and complex naval system for their age. *Shinobi* had to understand naval warfare and coastal geography in order to identify the best place for a fleet to dispatch its landing craft and deploy troops. The troops would need to be able to disembark safely, form a defensive position and then move inland.

Lesson 101

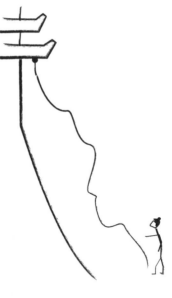

MEASURING A TOWER HEIGHT WITH A STICKY ARROW

This lesson comes from the *Bansenshūkai*. However, the original text is ambiguous so this is a hypothesis.

Move up to a fortification on a dark night with a bow, a length of thin cord and an arrow that has been dipped in a heavily sticky substance, such as tar. Tie the cord to the end of the "sticky arrow", then shoot it up to the underside of a turret. Once the arrow has stuck to the turret, gently pull the cord taut and mark where it touches the ground. Then pull harder on the cord to bring the arrow down. Back in the safety of camp, measure the distance between the arrow and the mark to give the height of the fortification. From here a tactician can construct ladders of the correct length and calculate the required trajectory of fire arrows and other siege weapons.

Lesson 102

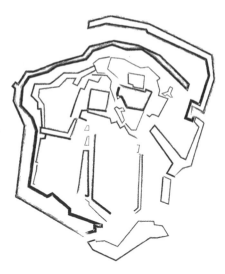

MAPPING OUT A CASTLE

Although there are regional variations, certain aspects of Japanese castle architecture are universal. Castles are constructed of concentric rings called *maru* (丸). These rings are not regular but follow the natural geography of the land. The gates, called *mon* (門), are not aligned with each other and are heavily defended. The pathways between the different rings weave and turn, each path being overlooked by arrow and gun ports. Attacking troops may make it through the outer gate only to enter the killing zone where they are faced with a complex system of paths and arcs of fire from arrows and guns.

The *shinobi*'s task is to map out a target castle in advance of an attack so that the commander knows the best way to approach it and so raiding troops are not confused by the layout on the other side of the gate. For this reason, in times of peace *shinobi* constantly build up diagrams of typical castle designs for each province.

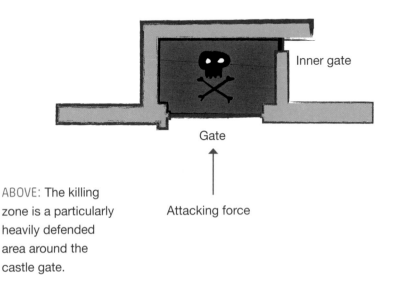

ABOVE: The killing zone is a particularly heavily defended area around the castle gate.

Lesson 103

OBSERVING BIRDS AROUND ENEMY TROOPS IN HIDING

To root out ambushes or enemy troops in hiding, stand before an area and observe the movement of birds. A noticeable lack of birds flying over a certain area or birds suddenly changing their course when they approach an area are both signs that soldiers may be concealed there.

Other signs to look out for include trodden-down pathways through grass and foliage, and accumulating smoke from fuses.

Shinobi **skill:** Any unnatural movement or flight patterns of birds can identify an enemy position.

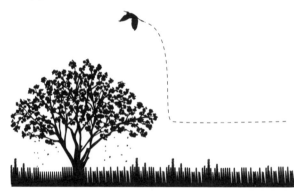

Lesson 104

OBSERVING BIRDS AROUND A CASTLE

Sometimes an enemy force may secretly flee its fortress under the cover of darkness, leaving the castle deserted or with only a skeleton crew to defend it. It is not easy to count the enemy on the battlements or observe their positions of defence by the naked eye alone, but you can gain valuable insights by observing the birds around castles. If birds perch on the walls with no fear and move along them without bursting into flight, or if they do not change their flight patterns as they approach the castle, this indicates that there are no

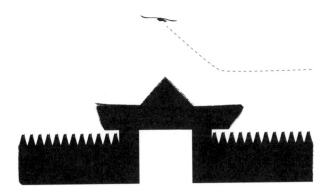

humans there. Conversely, birds suddenly moving off is a sign that humans are present.

Shinobi **skill:** The manuals also warn us that some types of bird gather around humans, for example to peck at dropped food. You need to understand the way different birds behave: giving a false report could have fatal consequences – not least for you.

Lesson 105

OBSERVING ENEMY FLAGS

While observing an enemy, a *shinobi* can pinpoint which groups contain the strongest troops. Remember that armies do not only consist of samurai; there are also mercenaries, semi-professional foot-soldiers and conscripts. A commander wishes to know which enemy troops are eager to fight and which are reluctant. One way to do this is to make observations of each group's flags. A group that is showing a readiness to fight will generally lean slightly forward and its flags will be angled markedly forward. In contrast, a group that is wanting to retreat will position itself slightly backwards, which will be clearly demonstrated by the angle of its flags.

Skills for capturing criminals

Lesson 106

CAPTURE WITH SPEED OR WITH PATIENCE

The term "criminal" is used in samurai Japan to refer not only to people who have committed a crime but also to those who have fallen out of favour with their lord. Once someone has been targeted for capture it is often the task of the *shinobi* to hunt them down. When handed a capture mission, you first need to find out the social status of your target, as this will help you to decide on the best approach. A samurai target will have learned the value of perseverance. Therefore, you should make the capture as quickly as possible because a samurai's resolve will not diminish over time. On the other hand, if the target is a non-samurai then it may be better to wait. Eventually the person's determination – being born in emotion – will fade and they will become lax, making their capture easier as time passes.

SAMURAI
Do not wait
to capture.

COMMON MAN
Wait to capture.

Lesson 107

BLOOD RELATIONS

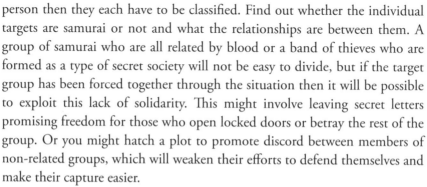

Building on the theme of the previous lesson, if the capture target consists of more than one person then they each have to be classified. Find out whether the individual targets are samurai or not and what the relationships are between them. A group of samurai who are all related by blood or a band of thieves who are formed as a type of secret society will not be easy to divide, but if the target group has been forced together through the situation then it will be possible to exploit this lack of solidarity. This might involve leaving secret letters promising freedom for those who open locked doors or betray the rest of the group. Or you might hatch a plot to promote discord between members of non-related groups, which will weaken their efforts to defend themselves and make their capture easier.

Issui-sensei delves deeper into capture skills in his scroll *Heika Jōdan* and discusses the various ways to capture a group defending a building, including coercion, fire attacks, infiltration, raiding parties and more.

Lesson 108

THE QUICK ROPE

Used to make a capture, the *hayanawa* quick rope is a thin but strong cord with a slender but robust hook on the end. Binding a target involves two basic steps: first, hook the target and restrain them with the quick rope and next use a stronger rope to bind them more securely for transport or imprisonment. Note that there are various rules and regulations on how to bind different people according to their social class.

Lesson 109

THE LEATHER BULLET

To capture a target without killing them, the *shinobi* use a special type of bullet that has a leather sleeve. Similar to the modern-day rubber bullet, the aim of this missile is to strike the target with a heavy blow, forcing them off balance or bringing them to their knees in shock so that the capture team can follow up and restrain them.

Lesson 110

USING POWDERS TO INCAPACITATE

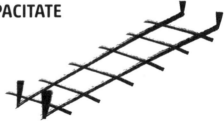

In samurai teaching there is a way known as *metsubushi*, which denotes the concoction of toxic powders designed to incapacitate an enemy by, for example, blinding or choking. One such powder consists of crushed blister beetles and arsenic. Blister beetles contain an irritant called cantharidin, which when ingested causes internal complications and possibly death if the dosage is high enough. Short-term exposure to arsenic can cause symptoms such as vomiting and disorientation.

A *shinobi* deploys this powder by wrapping it in paper (or a handkerchief) to form a small gas bomb. When unwrapping the paper before throwing a gas bomb toward the head of the target, the *shinobi* makes absolutely sure to be upwind so that none of the powder blows back. With the enemy incapacitated, the *shinobi* moves in to carry out the arrest or execution (covering their nose and mouth to avoid breathing in any of the powder).

Lesson 111

CHASING THE ENEMY WITH A SWORD OR SPEAR

When running after a fleeing target, there is a teaching that determines which side you should chase them on. If you are holding a spear you should run on the right side of the fugitive, whereas if you are holding a sword you should run on their left side. The reason is to do with ease of attack. A right-handed person will find it easier to thrust a spear to their left and cut with a sword to their right. Thrusting a spear to the right is more difficult because the shaft tends to hit your leg; and striking with a sword to the left means it has to cross your body in a backhand fashion, which is much weaker than a forehand strike. This advice is reversed if you are left-handed.

Lesson 112

POWDER-DIFFUSION DEVICES

Shinobi have many ingenious ways to store and deploy toxic powder. For example, it can be flicked out from a folded fan or whipped out of a secret compartment at the top of a cane, or loaded into an eggshell, which is then broken and thrown at the enemy when required.

Lesson 113

SHOOTING POWDER FROM A MUSKET

Fujibayashi-sensei prefers this method to those described in the previous two lessons, as the powder is propelled quite a long way. The *shinobi* rams the powder instead of a bullet into a musket, then pushes the musket through a window and fires it. The powder disperses through the room and begins to choke and blind the occupants, incapacitating them or making them run outside for air.

Lesson 114

THE WAY OF THE SWORD

Not all *shinobi* need to be highly skilled in hand-to-hand combat, as some are linguists, strategists, propaganda agents etc., but they do all need to have at least a basic understanding of swordsmanship. *Kenjutsu* (剣術) is the general term for skills with the sword and *iai* (居合) is the specific art of drawing the sword. *Kenjutsu* should be clinical and brutal and *iai* must be done with speed and accuracy.

When practising your sword skills, always favour effectiveness over elegance. The famed swordsman Miyamoto Musashi, who was writing in the 1640s, complained that the samurai of his time produced "more flowers than fruit", by which he meant that their arts looked beautiful but were impractical.

Shinobi **skill:** Students of *shinobi* ways should study the way of the sword and of quick draw, honing their skills until they are deadly, efficient and fearsome.

Lesson 115

CAPTURING BY FIRE

If a target group has successfully boarded itself inside a building, is defending it with skill and has shown no gaps to take advantage of, *shinobi* may have to resort to setting the building alight. Japan is famous for its wooden constructions and while they incorporate some fireproofing measures, they cannot easily be defended against a sustained fire attack. A classic *shinobi* tactic is to seal up all but one exit before setting fire to a building. This forces the people inside to exit from a single doorway, making them easy to capture or kill. (See also lesson 125.)

Fire
Skills

Lesson 116

STARTING FIRE

ABOVE: The basic fire triangle: heat, fuel and oxygen are the three things needed to start a fire.

While *shinobi* scrolls contain a large number of fire skills, they say very little about how to start a fire. To the modern reader this may seem odd, but the reason is obvious: at the time the scrolls were written everyone would have known how to start a fire naturally without special equipment, because this was the only way to do it.

However, one fire-starting tool the Japanese did carry was a special container for carrying embers from a previous fire.

Shinobi skill: To gain a pure and deep understanding of *shinobi* fire skills, reconnect with the old ways of creating fire and make sure you know how to start a fire in any given situation.

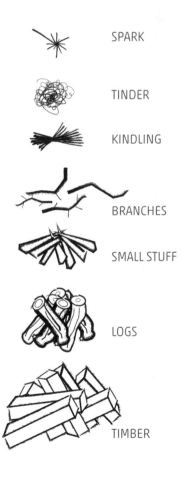

RIGHT: A fire needs to start small, with a spark, moving to tinder, then to kindling and then to larger pieces of fuel. Always make sure to prepare enough "small stuff" when trying to create fire in the wild.

153

Lesson 117

UNDERSTANDING FIRE

The *shinobi* are masters of *kajutsu* (火術) – the way of fire. The topic is complex and colossal, therefore each lesson on *kajutsu* should be considered as a small step toward a full understanding of how to use fire.

KAJUTSU

Some key terms:

- ignition – the starting of a fire
- combustion – the process of burning
- incendiary – that which ignites fires and burns with heat
- deflagration – the propagation of combustion from one substance to another at a subsonic velocity through heat transfer (e.g. a flash fire)
- detonation – the propagation of combustion at a supersonic velocity, causing a powerful shock wave

Types of burning:

- slow burning – oils, pitch, sulphur
- quick burning – liquid fire, naphtha, "Greek fire"
- explosion – gunpowder (also known as black powder)

Lesson 118

UNDERSTANDING GUNPOWDER

Among the *shinobi's* darker skills is arson (*hōka* in Japanese). *Shinobi* may be called upon to destroy a baggage train, castle, village, or even a whole town. Fundamental to such missions is gunpowder.

Some basic principles of gunpowder:

- Gunpowder is comprised of
  the following ingredients:
  saltpetre (75%), sulphur (15%)
  and charcoal (10%).
- Sulphur ignites at a relatively low
  temperature to start combustion.
- The burning of the sulphur raises
  the temperature high enough to
  ignite the saltpetre, which then
  expands dramatically.
- Gunpowder burns but does not explode when in the open. An explosion only
  occurs when gunpowder is ignited in a container.

Lesson 119

SETTING MULTIPLE FIRES AT THE SAME TIME

Shinobi work in a fire team to set fires simultaneously at multiple locations. Upon a given signal, such as the striking of the town hour bell, the agents set light at each of the locations. This is often done in conjunction with a night raid. However, any fire must be set with consideration of the wind and the direction from which the raid is going to occur. Sun Tzu warns that an attacking general does not want to be in the path of the smoke or the fire and an attacking troop needs to be upwind of a fire and not downwind.

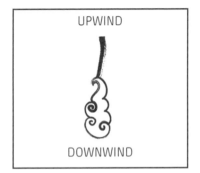

Lesson 120

KEEPING A FIRE BURNING IN RAIN

Most basic fires, if fed regularly with fuel, will continue to burn even in rain. However, the more it rains the more attention a fire needs and there will, of course, come a point where heavy rain kills even the most well-fed fire. Torches, because they are often left unattended, need to be able to stay alight in rain without being fed. They need to have fuel that creates enough heat to counter the water yet can also burn for a prolonged period. They may have components such as oils and resins that repel the water as the tar-like substance burns. Recipes for these waterproof torches are found in most *shinobi* scrolls, in particular the *Bansenshūkai*.

Lesson 121

THE ATTACK TORCH

SPIKE

TEAWHISK

CROSS BARS

The attack torch (*uchitaimatsu*) is distinguished by wooden cross bars or a metal spike attached to the base so that when the torch is thrown it lands upright. It is used to provide immediate illumination of an area that a *shinobi* squad is about to attack under cover of darkness.

Shinobi skill: A team approaches a target in the darkness, ignites torches, launches them and moves in to kill.

Lesson 122

THE SHIELD TORCH

Japan has two main types of shield: the *tate*, a freestanding wooden board supported by a single "leg" behind which a warrior will stand on an open battlefield; and the *tedate*, a handheld shield with a viewing port. The *tedate* is used by mounted scouts to protect against projectiles as they ride toward the enemy, while *shinobi* use it to corner criminals or to move forward toward the enemy in the dark. The *shinobi* version also has a candle-like torch on the front which is made of a compound that sets hard and burns well. One of the more famous depictions of the *tedate* shield is found in the 17th-century *Rōdanshū* scroll.

Shinobi skill: A warrior acting as a scout or *shinobi* must be able to wield a sword and a shield in unison, whether on horseback or on foot.

Lesson 123

HAND GRENADES

As discussed in lesson 64, the *shinobi* use hand grenades for shock and destruction. These are either clay spheres halved and then re-joined and wrapped in paper or they are made out of pliable lead. Both versions have a fuse. The *shinobi* ignite these and launch them into groups or buildings or anywhere else that the situation demands. When used in large numbers on a night raid they cause immense confusion and panic among the enemy.

Lesson 124

LANDMINES

The *shinobi* had a version of the landmine, which, while rudimentary by modern standards, was advanced for its time. It consists of a thin wooden box with gunpowder and stones inside and a fuse leading to the charge. The precise details of the fuse mechanism are unclear, but it would appear that the fuse is either timed with the approach of an enemy or activated by the weight of someone standing on it. In this second hypothesis, lit fuses are positioned on top of the thin box with shaved bamboo halves concealing them. When an enemy stands on the flimsy box the lid cracks and the burning fuse drops onto the gunpowder, which explodes, propelling the stones into the unprotected groin of the victim and any surrounding comrades.

Lesson 125

FIRE FOR CAPTURING PEOPLE

This tool is used for combat at close quarters when a criminal needs to be restrained. It consists of a handle and a tube, which is filled with a fast-burning fuel. When the fuel is lit it is forced out of a small opening. Arresting agents will light the tool before moving in on the enemy, while others make the capture.

Lesson 126

FIRE ON THE END OF A SPEAR

This tool is used when fighting a large number of enemy troops or for criminal capture. The tip of the spear carries a high-intensity fuel which is lit immediately before the spear is thrust toward the enemy. Natori-Ryū teaches samurai to use torches on the end of spears to capture or kill infiltrators.

Shinobi **skill:** Make sure that the enemy is downwind so that the smoke and flames are swept forward onto them.

Lesson 127

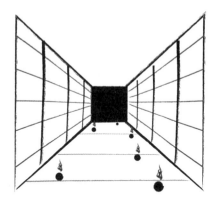

FIRE BALLS

There are two main types of fire ball: larger balls of compacted gunpowder and mixed iron filings, which are thrown; and smaller balls, which are rolled along the ground.

The first type burns at a high rate so that when it is thrown into an enemy group it will send troops scattering and produce gaps in their lines. The second type is used by *shinobi* on infiltration missions. They light it and gently roll it down a dark corridor for illumination. The ball does not set fire to the floor because the flame always stays on top.

Skills of Heaven

Lesson 128

A MAP OF THE STARS

The stars played an important role in pre-modern society and there would have been a much higher level of understanding among ordinary people of the "roof of the world" than there is now. In particular, the *shinobi* look to the stars to find their direction, to know the time and for astrological divination. Fujibayashi-sensei teaches that students of *shinobi* ways must have a map of the stars on a wall in their home so that they can learn to read the sky as if it were a book, a discipline known as *tenmongaku* (天文学).

Shinobi **skill:** Follow Fujibayashi's teaching – have a map of the stars upon the wall and study it to help you to read the sky, including:

- the constellations
- the movement of the heavens
- navigating by the stars
- telling the time through the stars
- the spiritual and religious significance of the stars

Lesson 129

THE OLD JAPANESE CALENDAR

A student of samurai ways should understand that the Japanese did not adopt the Gregorian calendar until 1873. Before then they followed the lunisolar Chinese calendar, which measured the year through observations of both the moon and the sun (the Gregorian calendar is purely solar). This system is undoubtedly complex and required a trained astronomer to devise any changes and insertions of dates. In an old *shinobi* manual when it gives a date as "the fourth day of the sixth month" know that this is not the fourth of June; it is, in fact, the fourth day of the sixth lunar month after the lunar new year (commonly known as Chinese New Year), which falls on a different date in the Gregorian calendar every year.

The lunar month is a division of time based on the moon and lasts approximately between 27 and 29 days, depending on how the moon is observed. The moon can be measured by its phases, or by its orbit or by its appearance in the sky.

Lesson 130

THE PHASES OF THE MOON

The moon is extremely important to the *shinobi* as it plays a large part in determining how dark or light a given night will be. To avoid detection, you will generally aim to infiltrate at the darkest phase of the lunar cycle – the new moon – although other factors may prevent this. The life of the *shinobi* is full of suspicion and uncertainty. The moon is one of the few things you can count on.

Bear in mind the following points when observing the moon:

- On a new moon the moon is fully black.
- On a full moon the moon is fully white.
- On a quarter moon the moon is half white, half black.
- During the waxing of the moon the area of light on the moon's surface gets larger.
- During the waning of the moon the area of light on the moon's surface gets smaller.
- On the moon all shadow and light moves from right to left.
- Like the sun, the moon rises at points in the east and sets at points in the west.
- The moon rises and sets 50 minutes later each day.

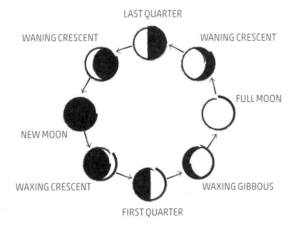

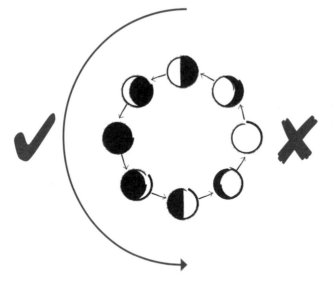

LEFT: This illustration helps a student of *shinobi* ways understand the lesson of Jizō and Yakushi. It shows the periods of dark nights, when one should infiltrate, and those of light nights, when one should not.

Lesson 131

INFILTRATING BETWEEN THE FESTIVALS OF JIZŌ AND YAKUSHI

"In principle, a shinobi *relies on darkness."*
Iga and Kōka Ninja Skills, Chikamatsu Shigenori, 18th century

As discussed in the previous lesson, a *shinobi* must pay careful attention to the passage of the moon and synchronize with its rhythms of light and dark. In medieval Japan the *shinobi* used two festivals held in each lunar month to mark the start of the waning and the waxing of the moon. One was dedicated to Jizō, a god for mothers who have lost children, which was held on the 24th day of the lunar month and was the point when the moonlight became lesser and the nights darker. The other festival, for Yakushi, a god of medicine, was held on the 8th day of the lunar month, which was when the moonlight started getting greater and the nights lighter. Therefore, the *shinobi* infiltrated during the 13 or 14 days after the festival of Jizō and before the festival of Yakushi, and castle commanders knew to be particularly vigilant during this time.

Lesson 132

THE SUN, THE MOON AND THE TIDES

Tides are the cyclical rising and falling of sea levels. They are governed by the gravitational forces exerted by the moon and sun and the rotation of the earth. The range between high tide and low tide is not constant. Spring tides, which occur when the earth, moon and sun are in alignment, are the most extreme – the high tide is at its highest and the low tide is at its lowest. Neap tides, which occur when the sun and the moon are at right angles to the earth, are the most moderate – the high tide is at its lowest and the low tide is at its highest.

Spring tides roughly coincide with the full moon and the new moon, while neap tides occur around seven days later, at the quarter stages of the moon (see image in lesson 84).

There is a short period of time between the tide coming in or going out when the water is in a state of equilibrium and there is no movement in either direction: this is known as still water or slack water.

Shinobi **skill:** *Shinobi* need to know when tides will be at their highest and lowest so that they do not, for example, send allied troops onto a beach when a spring tide is coming in.

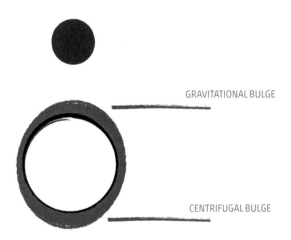

GRAVITATIONAL BULGE

CENTRIFUGAL BULGE

ABOVE: Both gravitational and centrifugal forces work on the tides.

Lesson 133

THE STAR OF DEFEAT

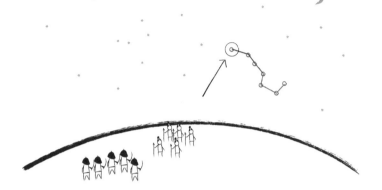

Certain stars were considered to be ominous or auspicious. For example, Hagun (Alkaid in Western astronomy), the last star in the "handle" of the Ursa Major constellation, was known by the samurai as the star of defeat. They believed that any army that fought in the direction of Hagun was destined to be defeated.

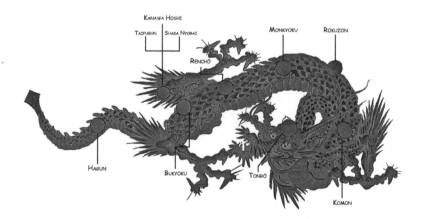

ABOVE: Ursa Major represented as a dragon with Venus attached. Image from the scrolls of Mubyōshi-Ryū.

Lesson 134

THE FOUR QUADRANTS OF THE SKY

In Chinese astrology-astronomy the sky is divided into four quadrants – east, south, west and north – each of which is associated with a supernatural animal and also has associations with the four seasons and the five elements (see lesson 2). This division of the sky dates back to prehistoric times and has been found on ancient tomb fragments. Like many other aspects of spirituality and philosophy, it travelled across the East China Sea to be assimilated in Japanese thinking. The table below summarizes how these aspects interact with each other. The *shinobi* would use these associations to plan their operations – for example, the most auspicious time, date and direction of infiltration.

Quadrant	Ideogram	Japanese	English (simplified)	Season	Element
East	青龍	Seiryū	Light blue dragon	Spring	Wood
South	朱雀	Suzaku	Scarlet bird	Summer	Fire
West	白虎	Byakko	White tiger	Autumn	Metal
North	玄武	Genbu	Black turtle	Winter	Water

Mystical Skills

Lesson 135

UNDERSTANDING ONMYŌDŌ

Onmyōdō is an esoteric thought system that covers a wide range of topics including divination, magic, astrology, the veneration of stars, animism (the belief that all objects have a soul), folk beliefs and ritual. Literally, the term means "the way of *yin* and *yang*" (陰陽道); however, the cultural weight behind each ideogram makes direct translation problematic. The origin of *onmyōdō* itself is difficult to trace, although some consider it to be the Japanese equivalent of organized Taoism. Most certainly it is based on Chinese thought – in particular, the deep mysteries of *yin* and *yang*.

Shinobi skill: A student of *shinobi* ways should understand the concept of *yin* and *yang* and the cycles of creation and destruction (see lessons 140 and 141). Furthermore, know that magic is found in many *shinobi* manuscripts and that *shinobi no jutsu* does contain ritual elements.

Lesson 136

THE GODDESS MARISHITEN

Marishiten is the Japanese version of the Buddhist goddess Marici, whose name literally means "mirage". She always travels in front of the sun, making her invisible, and she has the power to remove suffering from those who worship her. She is the basis for a form of invisibility magic called *ongyō* (隠形; see lesson 143).

Shinobi skill: Marishiten's association with invisibility makes her an obvious focus of worship for the *shinobi*. Many warriors have statues and altars in honour of her.

Lesson 137

CELEBRATING MARISHITEN

When warriors acquire new weapons they should celebrate by facing the direction of Marishiten and offering praise to her. To do this you need to identify the zodiac animal for that day and count the corresponding number of positions on the Chinese calendar.

Use the diagram and the following system to find the correct direction. The example in the diagram below is for the day of the rat. Count nine places clockwise around the circle, starting your counting on the day of the rat itself, and you will find that that you need to face in the direction of the monkey, ie. approximately southwest by west. The list below explains the system for the other days:

- On days of the rat, hare, horse and cockerel, count nine places around the calendar (to monkey, boar, tiger and snake respectively).
- On days of the ox, ram, dragon and dog, count five places around the calendar (to snake, boar, monkey and tiger respectively).
- On days of the tiger, monkey, snake and boar, you do not need to count any places: the direction of Marishiten is the same as the sign for that day.

Shinobi **skill:** There are 12 animals in the zodiac and the pre-modern Japanese week was 12 days long. To discover the animal of the day you can use an online Chinese calendar or app. Next count the direction and celebrate Marishiten.

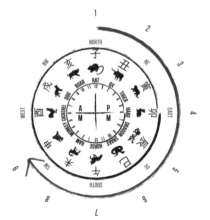

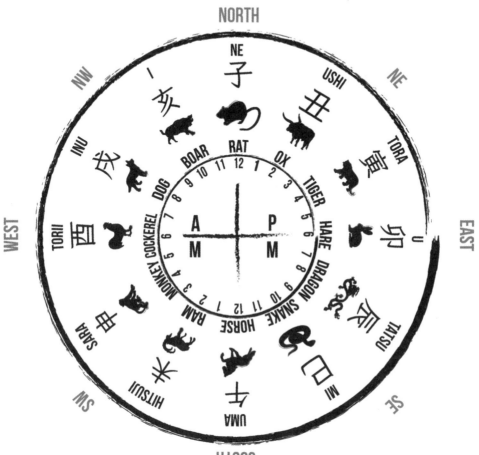

ABOVE: A chart for calculating lucky and unlucky directions.

OPPOSITE: A chart for calculating the direction of Marishiten.

Lesson 138

THE GODS OF WAR

It is said that there are 98,000 gods of war in Japan and that samurai must give reverence to each of these to assure victory in battle. However, Issui-sensei states that there is just one deity, named Miwa Daimyōjin, who takes the form of a snake with 98,000 scales on his body. This became the inspiration for the idea of there being 98,000 separate gods.

Shinobi **skill:** A student of samurai ways must understand that Japanese religion is polytheistic – meaning that it has many gods – and that for the Japanese warrior the gods of war are important in his spiritual journey. You must pursue a solid understanding of Japanese religion.

Early Buddhism	Zen
Reciting the Sutras	Meditation
Magic rituals	To clear the mind
Worship of the various Buddhas	To understand the mind of the Buddha

Lesson 139

CELEBRATING THE GODS OF WAR

On a given day in each lunar month warriors should perform prayers to the gods of war. Use a modern Chinese calendar in conjunction with the following list, a simplified version of the skill given in the *Bansenshūkai*, to find the correct day in each lunar cycle.

- In the first lunar month, it is on the day of the tiger.
- In the second lunar month, it is on the day of the hare.
- In the third lunar month, it is on the day of the snake.
- In the fourth lunar month, it is on the day of the ram.
- In the fifth lunar month, it is on the day of the cockerel.
- In the sixth lunar month, it is on the day of the boar.
- In the seventh lunar month, it is on the day of the hare.
- In the eighth lunar month, it is on the day of the snake.
- In the ninth lunar month, it is on the day of the ram.
- In the tenth lunar month, it is on the day of the cockerel.
- In the eleventh lunar month, it is on the day of the boar.
- In the twelfth lunar month, it is on the day of the hare.

Lesson 140

THE CYCLE OF CREATION

As the universe moves between *yin* and *yang*, the five elements of Wood, Fire, Earth, Metal and Water are produced. The process takes place in a particular order, which is known as the cycle of creation, or the generating cycle:

- Wood fuels fire.
- Fire produces ash and enriches the earth.
- Earth contains and produces metal.
- Metal collects water.
- Water nourishes wood …

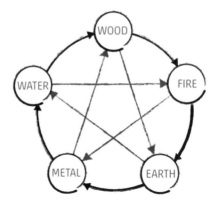

LEFT: A diagram showing the cycles of creation and destruction.

This simple process permeates all of samurai warfare and must be considered as an absolute foundation for study. One key factor to remember is that everything – including people, animals, objects, times and directions – has a core element. We are each fundamentally of Wood, Fire, Earth, Metal or Water, depending on the time and date of our birth, and we need to associate ourselves with things whose core element complements our own to ensure that we are in a generating-creative relationship with our surroundings. Even the bamboo that a samurai uses as a banner pole is connected to one of the five elements and that element must align with the element of the samurai who uses it. Also consider the horse a samurai rides; it too must match the element of the samurai.

In short, *yin* and *yang* form the world, the movement of *yin* and *yang* forms the five elements, and those five elements react with each other in all aspects of life.

***Shinobi* skill:** When planning any undertaking a *shinobi* must weigh up both practical logic and the mystical cycle of creation.

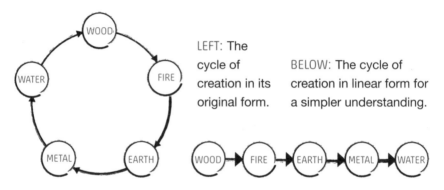

LEFT: The cycle of creation in its original form.

BELOW: The cycle of creation in linear form for a simpler understanding.

Lesson 141

THE CYCLE OF DESTRUCTION

The cycle of destruction describes a negative, controlling process, in contrast to the positive, generative process of the cycle of creation:

* Wood churns up the earth.
* Earth soaks up water.
* Water extinguishes fire.
* Fire melts metal.
* Metal hacks at wood …

The cycle of destruction shows how one element has control over another. If a samurai uses the wrong piece of bamboo, rides the wrong horse, or attacks from the wrong direction on the wrong day, then a negative energy will prevail.

Shinobi **skill:** A *shinobi* student should fully understand the cycle of destruction and be aware of the negative effects it can have.

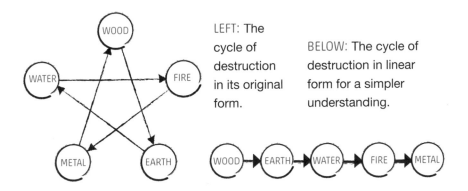

LEFT: The cycle of destruction in its original form.

BELOW: The cycle of destruction in linear form for a simpler understanding.

Lesson 142

DISPLAYING DECAPITATED HEADS

Even the displaying of decapitated heads must be done in harmony with the five elements. Although this is not generally considered to be part of *shinobi no jutsu*, Fujibayashi-sensei discusses it in the *Bansenshūkai*. After warriors have taken a head as proof of a kill, the head must then be gibbeted in the correct direction. They start by taking the animal zodiac for that day and then gibbet the head in the direction stipulated below. For example, on a day of the rat a head must be placed in the direction of the horse, which is due south (see the chart in lesson 137).

- On a day of the rat, gibbet the head in the direction of the horse.
- On a day of the ox, gibbet the head in the direction of the snake.
- On a day of the tiger, gibbet the head in the direction of the monkey.
- On a day of the hare, gibbet the head in the direction of the dragon.
- On a day of the dragon, gibbet the head in the direction of the snake.
- On a day of the snake, gibbet the head in the direction of the horse or ram.
- On a day of the monkey, gibbet the head in the direction of the snake.
- On a day of the cockerel, gibbet the head in the direction of the ram.
- On a day of the dog, gibbet the head in the direction of the monkey.
- On a day of the boar, gibbet the head in the direction of the tiger.

The gibbeting direction for days of the horse and ram are not specified.

Shinobi skill: Fujibayashi-sensei tells us that a head must never be placed in the direction of Hagun, the star of defeat (see lesson 133). If the star appears in the direction stipulated for that day, a *shinobi* should hold off until a day when the direction no longer corresponds to Hagun or seek the advice of a *gunbaisha*, an esoteric tactician.

Lesson 143

MAGICAL HIDING

Ongyō (隠形) is a set of spells and beliefs connected to the goddess of war, Marishiten (see lessons 136 and 137). In keeping with Marishiten's association with invisibility, *ongyō* spells tend to focus on ways to make yourself invisible. They are not unique to the *shinobi*, but the *shinobi* use them along with other similar spells while on missions.

THE ONGYŌ SPELL

This is known as *ongyō no ju* (隠形の呪), the "spell of invisibility". The original spell came from India and the Japanese changed the pronunciation. Having hidden your face behind your sleeve (see lesson 39), chant the following spell to yourself in your mind:

On anichi marishi ei sowaka

LEFT: These ideograms represent the *ongyō* spell. They are not part of mainstream Buddhism and should be seen as a variation of the ritual of *ongyō*. The calligraphy was written by Monk Jyuhō Yamamoto.

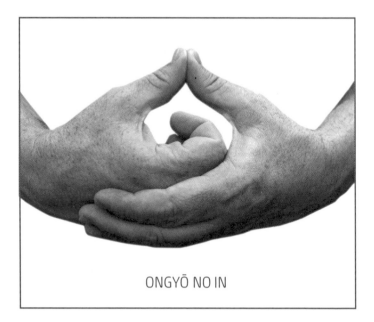

ONGYŌ NO IN

ABOVE: The *mudra* of *ongyō no in*.

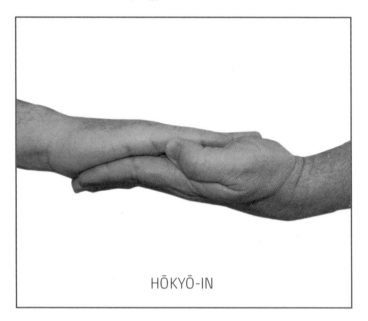

HŌKYŌ-IN

ABOVE: The *mudra* for the *Bansenshūkai* version of the *ongyō* ritual. In this case the *mudra* is *hōkyō-in* (宝篋印), which is dedicated to Kan'non, the Buddhist goddess of mercy.

THE MUDRA OF HIDING

A *mudra* is a symbolic hand gesture commonly used in Hinduism and Buddhism. The *mudra* of invisibility, *ongyō no in* (隠形の印), represents the sun and the moon, symbols of Marishiten, and also the idea of hiding itself. The fist is the sun and the open hand the moon. Place the open palm of one hand to the side of the fist of the other hand or over the top of it.

By using all three elements – hiding behind their sleeve, silent chanting of the spell, and performing the *mudra* – *shinobi* are said to render themselves invisible to the enemy.

Magical hiding from the lore of the *shinobi* is a long and complex story with multiple variations. The above is taken from the *Bansenshūkai* and is just one of many systems.

Skills of
the Mind

Lesson 144

BRUTE COURAGE VERSUS COURAGE OF DUTY

Courage can come from three sources: discipline, emotion and intoxication. (Understand that courage through intoxication exists, but discard it as an option for the *shinobi*.)

The *Bansenshūkai* discusses the concepts of courage of duty and brute courage. To have courage of duty is to be centred, to have discipline, training and education and turn it into bravery, whereas brute courage is founded on natural strength and hot-blooded emotion. Both can be enormously powerful, but brute courage does not last as it relies on natural strength, which when pushed to its limit will break, and hot-bloodedness, which soon cools. In contrast, courage of duty lasts throughout all situations. This is because it is based on the concept of *dōshin*, the "mind of principles", which is unwavering, while brute courage comes from *jinshin*, the "mind of man", which is changeable. These two concepts are explained in the following lesson.

Lesson 145

THE CONCEPTS OF JINSHIN AND DŌSHIN

"Though a man's mind and heart are simply his mind and heart, there are in fact two types of this central being. There is jinshin *(人心), the 'mind of man', and* dōshin *(道心), the 'mind of principle', and the latter is understood as having an affinity to what is right."*

Bansenshūkai, Fujibayashi-sensei, 1676

Jinshin and *dōshin* should be understood as two voices conducting an internal dialogue in the mind:

- *Jinshin* is the lower voice that persuades us to do what benefits us in the short term but may be harmful to the greater good.
- *Dōshin* is the higher voice telling us an action is not correct and that it is better to do what is right.

As Fujibayashi-sensei describes it, *jinshin* "is easily affected by what the eye sees, worries about what the ear hears, is absorbed in what the nose smells, indulges in the five tastes and allows the body to give in to lust". It is a powerful force, because we are all conditioned to do what we can to satisfy our immediate self-interest.

In contrast, according to Fujibayashi-sensei those with *dōshin* "will not give heed to anything unrighteous and if they see lust in someone's eyes, or if they hear others they will let it pass. They do not do anything that is not righteous itself or not respectful and will not indulge in negativity. If you do not pay attention to your own desire despite your self-interest and follow your righteous nature and have no selfishness, then it can be said that in this way, you act with the mind of principle."

Note that *dōshin* is inextricably linked to the Taoist concept of the Way (see lesson 10). It can be read as meaning "an aspiration to follow the Way". The concept of *dōshin* was prevalent in medieval Japan and adherents to this idea formed into a subclass of their own. The term *dōshinja* (sometimes *dōshinsha*) denoted a form of lesser-priest who would wander between communities or take up a hermitage, receiving money from local believers to perform rites and administer spiritual aid – to the annoyance of the sanctioned religious orders. Fujibayashi-sensei does not intend students of the *shinobi* arts to adopt such a regime, but he certainly teaches us to aspire to follow the Way.

Shinobi **skill:** Learn to check your internal dialogue and recognize whether what your mind is telling you to do is for your own benefit or for the greater good.

Lesson 146

OBSERVING THE INNER MIND

Following on from the previous two lessons, *shinobi* are required to constantly practise mental self-diagnostics, to be unflinchingly honest about their own thoughts and motivations.

Use the following guidelines:

- Place the mind of principle (harsh honesty) in control.
- Truthfully identify the influence of the mind of man (self-deception).
- Self-deception and desire should always give way to harsh and true honesty.
- Harsh and true honesty should be lord above all things.
- This is not an external battle, as the enemy is in our own mind.

If we follow these guidelines closely, Fujibayashi-sensei promises us that: "The mind of principle will come out as clearly as the moon comes out from behind the clouds."

Lesson 147

DETACHING FROM LIFE AND DEATH

One of the essential components of Buddhist study is understanding that death is an illusion, just part of the cycle of death and rebirth (see lesson 7). For the Taoist the concept of *wu-wei* (*mui* in Japanese) means to not go against the grain, to allow nature to flow and to engage with whatever the universe presents to you, no matter whether it is negative or positive. Such ways of thinking, achieved only after deep spiritual study, are what enable the *shinobi* to face even the most dangerous situations with a calm, clear mind.

Issui-sensei says that life is found within death, meaning that even when a situation seems sure to end in your death you should engage with it and push through, because often survival is found in brave actions instead of the lesser actions of self-preservation. Natori-Ryū teachings also state that a *shinobi* should "detach from the two swords of life and death". Most people, if they are honest, would panic if faced with the prospect of death. However, by making a sustained effort to cultivate a disciplined and honest mind, a student of *shinobi* ways can develop a new level of natural confidence and ability.

Lesson 148

KNOWING WHEN TO TELL THE TRUTH AND WHEN TO LIE

Although the *shinobi* are known as masters of deception, they should lie very rarely. Certainly, when not engaged in *shinobi* activity it would be disgraceful for a *shinobi* to lie, as dishonesty is against the warrior's code. Even when operating undercover, *shinobi* should tell the truth as often as possible, or steer as close to it as their undercover persona will allow them, in order to build a solid foundation and establish their credibility with the enemy. This even extends to revealing relatively trivial facts that will give the enemy small advantages over the *shinobi's* true lord. It is only when a plan is about to bloom that the *shinobi* tells a momentous lie to bring down the enemy.

Shinobi **skill:** A *shinobi* is a person whom the lord knows he can trust, and whom the enemy lord believes he can trust – until it is too late.

Lesson 149

THE WAY OF STUDY

To help the next generation of *shinobi* students to grow in the correct manner, a set of guidelines must be established and they should be considered as a cornerstone for all those serious in their *shinobi* training.

CHOOSING THE RIGHT SCHOOL

If you are considering taking up formal study of *shinobi no jutsu*, avoid those organizations that call themselves a "ninja school" or claim to teach *only* the arts of the ninja. Look instead for a school that promotes itself as a *gungaku* ("school of military study"), and uses terms such as: *gundō* (軍道), "military ways"; *gunjutsu* (軍術), "military skills"; and *heihō* (兵法), "the ways of the soldier". It is fine to choose a school that teaches the arts of the *shinobi* as part of its full samurai curriculum. However, a school that promotes itself as teaching only *ninjutsu* shows a lack of understanding – it is in essence informing people that it is incomplete.

A modern-day student of the *shinobi* arts should have a foundation in Japanese martial arts, strategy, warfare, philosophy, religion, literature, culture, history and magic, as well as in Chinese culture, literature, military tactics and history. By developing this richness of understanding you will give yourself every chance of flourishing into an excellent student, and perhaps even a future master.

CHOOSING THE RIGHT EQUIPMENT

Students should not train in modern karate uniforms with karate belts or follow the modern system of *dan* grades. Formal training should be done in a *kimono* and *hakama* with an *obi* belt and with a long sword and a short sword. Martial arts training should be done in a *kimono* with sleeve ties (*tasuki*) or with a *dōgi* training top. Any systems of grading should be in accordance with historical ways (see lesson 18). When training outdoors wear clothing suited to the conditions. Modern but simple trekking or combat gear is acceptable; traditional Japanese harsh weather equipment is even better. All equipment should be suited to the environment, whether it be formal or casual, and should reflect the essence of the time.

Lesson 150

THE WAY OF FULL UNDERSTANDING

Modern students of *shinobi no jutsu* must understand that the *shinobi* died out long ago. To be a *shinobi* one would need to have been alive in Japan before 1868, which is impossible. But while we can no longer be genuine *shinobi*, there is no reason why we cannot genuinely study their ways and model our understanding of the world on their teachings.

Never forget that you are a product of modern times. This is not a step into fantasy, but a way to redefine your mode of thinking and build a disciplined character. It is a journey to realize your potential. The way of the *shinobi* is the way of full understanding.

Shinobi Scrolls

Reading Shinobi Scrolls

Many scrolls may contain the term *shinobi* but this does not make them *shinobi* scrolls. Consider a *shinobi* scroll as a manuscript that primarily focuses on teaching the arts of the ninja, and whose contents were written by an active *shinobi* or someone initiated into the teachings during the samurai period.

There is a relative abundance of *shinobi* scrolls in the world, and not only in Japan. Some are held in public library collections, some in private institutes and others in the hands of individual collectors. To date there has been no comprehensive cataloguing of the world's *shinobi* scrolls. However, it is clear that most were written during the Edo period (*c.*1603–1868). Some independent lists claim to contain scrolls that predate 1603, but these works have never been published, with the exception of Hattori Hanzo's *Shinobi Hiden* (1560).

The date of 1603 is of great importance because it saw the consolidation of power in Japan under the Tokugawa family and brought an end to the civil wars of the preceding Sengoku period. This means that any work that predates 1603 or one that is within a few decades after this date is likely to have been written by someone who lived through or even fought in Japan's warring period, giving it a level of first-hand credibility. In fact, most of what we know about the historical *shinobi* comes from writers who lived during a time of peace and did not themselves see active service. However, these writers would have been privy to the secrets of *shinobi no jutsu* and, in some cases, had direct contact with war-tested *shinobi*.

LEVELS OF ACCESSIBILITY

Pre-modern Japanese literature is mysterious, guarded and sometimes impregnable, and *shinobi* writings can be some of the most unfathomable. However, manuals such as the *Bansenshūkai*, the *Shōninki*, the *Yōkan* series and the *Gunpō Jiyōshū* offer a more open approach, having been written by extremely forward-thinking individuals whose aim was primarily preservation not secrecy.

Shinobi scrolls can be categorized according to their accessibility, from the most enigmatic to the most descriptive.

LEVEL 1 – ENIGMATIC

Mokuroku (目録) are untitled scrolls consisting of lists of skill names or memory hooks. They were used as instructional aids, but not intended for posterity: a teacher would discuss each topic on the list and pass on their meanings through *kuden* (口傳), "oral tradition". In some cases later students have recorded such oral tradition in commentaries; all such commentaries should be considered as recorded oral tradition.

LEVEL 2 – INSIGHTFUL

Some scrolls list skills and also give some hints at how the skills were used. These normally comprise a list of titles with a small section on the traditions described in the scroll.

ABOVE: A section of the *Shinobi Taimatsu* scroll showing a simple list of titles. Without oral tradition or commentary the meanings can only be guessed at.

LEVEL 3 – DESCRIPTIVE

Some scrolls were written with the intention of capturing and maintaining the ways of the *shinobi* for future generations. These have full explanations that leave only the problem of our contextual understanding and archaic vocabulary to deal with and the occasional missing point that has not been passed down in oral tradition.

ABOVE: The *Bansenshūkai* is the most descriptive *shinobi* scroll and contains an enormous number of secrets – the edition shown here is a modern facsimile. The full scroll is translated in *The Book of Ninja* (Watkins, 2013).

COMMON MISCONCEPTIONS

Be careful not to fall into the following traps when studying *shinobi* scrolls:

- The scrolls do not contain all a person needs to know to be a *shinobi*. Many non-*shinobi* skills are needed to be a successful agent. *Shinobi* scrolls add the clandestine skills required to turn a conventional warrior into a special agent.
- *Shinobi* scrolls are not written in code. Because many of the names in skill lists can sound poetic, people wrongly believe they are in code. There are only a very few examples of ciphers being used to encode ninja skills.
- Although general Japanese warfare manuals draw extensively on the Chinese military classics, this is not so true of the *shinobi* scrolls. Japanese culture during the time of the *shinobi* was heavily influenced by China and so it was fashionable to show an understanding of the Chinese classics. Therefore, the writers of *shinobi* scrolls did sometimes quote from Chinese literature to demonstrate the value of a skill by connecting it to a Chinese antecedent. However, there are many skills of the *shinobi* that are not based on the Chinese classics.
- The contents of the scrolls should not be dismissed as "medieval madness". It is true that many *shinobi* scrolls contain strange spells and teachings that are clearly incorrect from a modern standpoint, but it must not be forgotten that in all medieval cultures, magic and mysticism were believed to be powerful forces and just because an occult skill does not in fact work does not mean it was not used or believed to be effective.

Military Tactics and the Seven Military Classics

Chinese Warfare

Working deep in enemy territory, with extremely limited means of communication back to his allies, the *shinobi* had to be able to think like a general. As the situation was evolving around him, he had to predict his army commander's intention at all times and act accordingly. Therefore, if you wish to inhabit the mind of the *shinobi* you will need not only to be well versed in the particular arts of the *shinobi* but also to have a general grounding in medieval Japanese warfare. This means having a solid foundation in Chinese military writings as well as their Japanese counterparts.

Each school (*ryū*) claimed to have its own brand of warfare, but variations were comparatively minor. (Only a handful of leaders in Japanese military history stand out as being particularly innovative; these include Kusunoki Masashige and Lord Oda Nobunaga.) Therefore, a student of Japanese warfare and the *shinobi* arts should start with the Seven Military Classics of China and then proceed to an individual school of *gungaku* ("military study").

The table below presents the Seven Military Classics of China (武經七書, Bukei Shichi Sho).

	Chinese ideograms	Chinese (simplified	Japanese	English (titles change depending on the translator and system used)
1	六韜	T'ai Kung Liu-t'ao (sometimes just Liu-t'ao)	Rikutō	T'ai Kung's Six Secret Teachings
2	司馬法	Ssu-ma Fa	Shibahō	The Methods of Ssu-ma (sometimes Sima)
3	孫子兵法	Sun Tzu (sometimes Sunzi)	Sonshi no Heihō	Sun Tzu's Art of War
4	吳子	Wu-tzu (sometimes Wuzi)	Goshi	Wu-tzu
5	尉繚子	Wei Liao-tzu	Utsuryōshi	Wei Liao-tzu
6	黃石公三略	Huang Shígong San Lue	Kōsekikō Sanryaku	The Three Strategies of Huang Shih-kung (sometimes Shigong)
7	唐太宗李衛公問對	Tang Taizong Li Wei Gong Wen Dui	Tō Taisō Rieikō Montai	Questions and Replies between T'ang T'ai-tsung and Li Wei-kung

ABOVE: Sun Tzu's *The Art of War* is known in Japanese as Sonshi no Heihō.

SUN TZU'S FIVE CONSTANT FACTORS

The most famous of the Seven Military Classics is Sun Tzu's *The Art of War*. This work can be considered as a foundation text for all warfare in Japan. The central element of *The Art of War* is the Five Constant Factors.

According to Sun Tzu, war has Five Constant Factors that must be, assessed, deliberated and compared:

1   The Way (道)
2   The heavens (天)
3   The earth (地)
4   The commander (将)
5   The organization and discipline of the force (法)

Military commanders cannot be successful without fully absorbing these factors into their planning. The Five Constant Factors are also fundamental to *shinobi* activities, as an agent has to be in harmony with a warlord so plans can flow effectively.

THE WAY

The Way can be seen as the Taoist Way (see lesson 10), which is the primary and immanent force that holds the universe together, but here it is perhaps meant more in the sense of moral ways and harmony. From a student of war's standpoint, this means knowing whether there is corruption or justice in both the allied and enemy forces. Is the leader honest? Are the laws fixed and is there true justice and wellbeing in the society as a whole, for both the high- and low-born? Corrupt, unfair and inhumane rulers are often hated and may have difficulty leading the masses.

When the Way is respected, the following happens:

- People join in harmony and have one mind.
- They are in tune with and supportive of their ruler.
- They will live and die for the state.
- They will stand firm.

Shinobi **skill:** An enemy force under a bad ruler will easily crumble and fall. However, if the ruler is fair and just, the force will fight with determination. In order to unbalance a balanced enemy, a *shinobi* must sow discord through propaganda.

THE HEAVENS

Here "heaven" means climate and weather and has no spiritual connotations. Generals and *shinobi* need to be able to forecast the weather and understand the effect that bad or good conditions have on terrain and on troops. Soldiers who are too hot, too wet or too cold do not function at their best. When entering enemy territory a commander must understand the climate there and plan accordingly.

Shinobi **skill:** The climate in a different region may be completely different from what you are used to and may vary drastically from one season to the next. It is the task of the *shinobi* to become skilled in meteorology so that they can report such matters to the commander.

THE EARTH

"Earth" in modern terms means geography and topography. A general cannot form functioning plans without detailed information on matters such as the type of ground, possible escape routes and the gradients of hills and mountains. Scouting, cartography and observation of the landscape with a military mind are among the *shinobi's* most important duties.

Understanding the earth means knowing the following:

- Where are the highest mountains and the deepest valleys? (Forces may be more vulnerable in these locations.)
- Is the enemy near or far?
- Is the ground heavy-going or easy to cover? (Difficult ground will stop vehicles and mounted troops and hamper the distribution of supplies.)
- Is the ground open and free or is it tight and confined? (For example, narrow passes carry the risk of an ambush.)

Shinobi skill: When scouting, a *shinobi* is thinking about the movement of the whole army through an area, not just an individual. That is why a *shinobi* should be able to calculate areas of land and assess whether an army can take up position there. An agent always considers the big picture.

THE COMMANDER

A strong military commander is the key to victory in warfare. Such a leader is one who has mastered war on behalf of the people and the troops. Being a good military commander requires the following qualities:

- wisdom and intelligence – to make detailed plans and be able to change them to outwit the enemy
- integrity – to inspire loyalty in the forces
- compassion – to understand when the forces are in discomfort and pain and to find a solution
- courage – to provide an example to the forces and to intimidate the enemy
- discipline – to have strict codes that are fair, to reward the true and punish the wrongdoer, and to show no favouritism to any individual or any rank

Shinobi skill: It can be difficult for the allied commander to move against an enemy leader who demonstrates all of these virtues. However, be aware that there are false versions of these qualities – they have to be genuine to be effective.

THE ORGANIZATION AND DISCIPLINE OF THE FORCE

The single ideogram for this factor, 法, is hard to translate directly into English, but Sun Tzu uses it to refer to military laws and codes, punishments and rewards, and discipline within the ranks of any force.

In short, a commander needs to take firm control of the following:

- organization – everybody knows where they should be and what they should be doing (as well as where they should not be and what they should not be doing)
- chain of command – there is a defined hierarchy and reporting structure so that every soldier knows who to inform if there is a problem
- logistics – supplies and equipment flow steadily so that a force is never left short of what it needs to function at its best

Shinobi **skill:** *Shinobi* scrolls devote a great deal of attention to mundane elements such as rations, laws and command structures. These may not seem particularly interesting to the modern reader, but they are essential in building up a full picture of the enemy. By discovering how the enemy runs its everyday operations, a *shinobi* can work out how to disrupt them.

SUN TZU'S 13TH CHAPTER

The Art of War comprises 13 chapters, each dedicated to a different aspect of warfare. The final chapter, entitled *"Yōkan"* (用間), deals with the use of spies. Japanese military espionage was clearly influenced by this chapter and the *shinobi* used it as a cornerstone of their tactics. Chikamatsu Shigenori, the military tactician who compiled *Iga and Kōka Ninja Skills*, included a massive amount of material from Sun Tzu's 13th chapter and Sun Tzu is often mentioned in Japanese military manuals and *shinobi* scrolls.

Any student of *shinobi no jutsu* should hold Sun Tzu's 13th chapter in high esteem and study it with fervour, but bear in mind that it covers only one strand of *shinobi* skills: those relating to classic spycraft. Some researchers have dismissed *shinobi no jutsu* as nothing more than a copy or pastiche of Sun Tzu, but, as the following breakdown will show you, there are many areas of *shinobi* arts, such as infiltration, burglary, disguise, fire, explosives and moat crossing, that the chapter does not cover.

An overview of Sun Tzu's 13th chapter:

- War is an expensive venture.
- War is a drain on the people.
- War is a drain on the economy.
- War disrupts the land.
- War can last for an unknown amount of time.
- War is a disturbance to all.
- Be generous to spies to gain information.
- Information and knowledge brings victory.
- Information cannot be obtained from spirits and divination.
- Information from analogy is insufficient.
- Information from estimation is insufficient.
- Useful information is acquired only from people who know the enemy situation.
- There are five types of spy:
    1 local spies – recruited from enemy population
    2 internal spies – recruited from enemy ranks
    3 double agents – recruited from enemy spies
    4 doomed spies – allied spies fed misinformation
    5 living spies – allied spies who return from missions
- Using the five types of spy together in combination makes for exquisite intelligence operations.
- No one is closer to a leader than his spies.
- Spies are rewarded richly.
- An unwise leader will not use spies correctly.
- An inhumane or unjust leader will not use spies correctly.
- An unsubtle leader will not discover the truth of a spy's report.
- Spies have innumerable uses.
- A spy who divulges information to others must be executed.
- When striking an army, attacking a city or plotting an assassination, spies gather information such as the names and positions of key people in enemy ranks.
- It is fundamental to uncover enemy spies.
- Bribe and richly reward enemy spies to turn them into double agents.
- Double agents can tell you who to recruit as local spies and internal spies.
- A leader must understand the five types of spy.
- A leader understands that spies are the key to a victorious military campaign.
- The movements of an entire army are governed by information that is gathered by spies.

SELECTED BIBLIOGRAPHY

Bell, D. A. (editor), *Confucian Political Ethics*, Princeton University Press, 2008.

Bellah, R., *Tokugawa Religion: The Cultural Roots of Modern Japan*, The Free Press, 1957.

Bowring, R., *The Religious Traditions of Japan 500–1600*, Cambridge University Press, 2005.

Bunce, W. K., *Religions in Japan: Buddhism, Shinto and Christianity*, Charles E. Tuttle Company, 1955.

Campion, N., *Astrology and Cosmology in the World Religions*, NYU Press, 2012

Cocroft, W. D., *Dangerous Energy: The Archaeology of Gunpowder and Military Explosives Manufacture*, English Heritage, 2000.

Como, M., *Weaving and Binding: Immigrant Gods and Female Immortals in Ancient Japan*, Hawaii University Press, 2009.

Cummins, A. and Y. Minami, *The Book of Ninja: The Bansenshukai, Japan's Premier Ninja Manual*, Watkins, 2013.

Cummins, A. and Y. Minami, *The Book of Samurai: Secret Teachings of Natori-Ryū*, Watkins, 2015.

Cummins, A. and Y. Minami, *True Path of the Ninja: The Definitive Translation of the Shōninki*, Tuttle, 2011.

Hall, D. A., *Encyclopedia of Japanese Martial Arts, Kodansha*, 2012.

Hayashi, M. and M. Hayter, "*Onmyōdō* in Japanese History", *Japanese Journal of Religious Studies* 40.

Ho, P. Y., *Chinese Mathematical Astrology*, Routledge, 2003.

Inagaki, H., *A Dictionary of Japanese Buddhist Terms: Based on References in Japanese Literature*, Nagata Bunshodo, 1984.

Japan Culture Institute, *A Hundred Things Japanese*, Japan Culture Institute, 1975.

Joseph, M., *The Wisdom of China*, Michael Joseph Ltd, 1944.

Kasahara, K., *A History of Japanese Religion*, Kosei Publishing, 2001.

Kawashima, C., *Minka: Traditional Houses of Rural Japan*, Kodansha, 1986.

Kitagawa, J. M., *Religion in Japanese History*, Columbia University Press, 1966.

Kornicki, P. F. and I. J. McMullen, *Religion in Japan: Arrows to Heaven and Earth*, Cambridge University Press, 1996.

Needham, J., *Science and Civilization in China*, Volume 5 Part 7, Cambridge University Press, 1986.

Needham, J., *Shorter Science and Civilization in China*, Volume 1, Cambridge University Press, 1978.

Needham, J., *Shorter Science and Civilization in China*, Volume 2, Cambridge University Press, 1981.

Penny, B. (editor), *Daoism in History: Essays in Honour of Liu Ts'un-yan*, Routledge, 2006.

Rigden, D. (editor), *SOE Syllabus*, Public Record Office, St Edmundsbury Press, 1988.

Saso, M. R., *Taoism and the Rite of Cosmic Renewal*, Washington State University Press, 1972.

Sawyer, R., *The Seven Military Classics of China*, Westview Press, 1993.

Wilkinson, J., *The Moon in Close-up*, Springer Publishing, 2010.

Yusa, M., *Japanese Religions*, Laurence King Publishing, 2002.

INDEX

ACKNOWLEDGEMENTS

I would like to thank above all Yoshie Minami
for her groundbreaking work in the study of the
Japanese *shinobi* – without her formidable efforts I
would still be wandering aimlessly in the darkness of
myth and hearsay. She is and should be recognized
as the true saviour of the Japanese *shinobi*. Next for
praise and adoration is Mieko Koizumi, the stalwart
"super-elf" who hides below giant and gnarled
writing desks, waiting to be handed tasks written
on aged parchment. Glory must be bestowed on the
artists Andrija Dreznjak and Jayson Kane, who have
worked beyond the call of duty to bring about such
excellent images; pictures which contain myself and
Paul Myers. Finally, thanks to Michael Mann, who
brought about this book and supported historical
shinobi no jutsu from the start.

Antony Cummins

ABOUT THE AUTHOR

Antony Cummins is an author and historical researcher, as well as leading the "resurrection" of the samurai school of war Natori-Ryū. He concentrates on investigating and disseminating the history of the Japanese *shinobi*. As project manager with the Historical Ninjutsu Research Team, Antony has overseen the translation and publication of multiple *shinobi* and samurai manuals, including: *The Book of Ninja, The Book of Samurai, Iga and Kōka Ninja Skills, The Secret Traditions of the Shinobi, True Path of the Ninja, The Lost Samurai School* and *Samurai War Stories.*

Antony has also published his own writing: two books on the samurai and *shinobi, In Search of the Ninja and Samurai* and *Ninja*; and a look at the darker side of Japanese folklore called *The Dark Side of Japan*. He has appeared in the TV documentaries *Samurai Headhunters, Ninja Shadow Warriors, Samurai Warrior Queens, The 47 Ronin* and *Ninja*.

For more information about Antony and his team, see current social media sites and his website: *www.natori.co.uk*

ABOUT THE ARTISTS

Andrija Dreznjak was born in Serbia and graduated from the University of Niš after studying Law. He has worked with Antony Cummins on several projects, including *Secrets of the Ninja* and *The Lost Samurai School*. He lives in Serbia and works as a freelance sculptor, graphic designer, comic book artist and script writer for graphic novels.

Jayson Kane is a freelance illustrator based in Manchester, UK, as well as working as a graphic designer in the textile industry. He was born in South Africa and studied Art, Design and Print Making in Manchester. Having worked with Antony Cummins for many years, Jayson's portfolio includes: *True Path of the Ninja* (cover concept designer), *The Secret Traditions of the* Shinobi (front cover designer), *Iga and Kōka Ninja Skills* (internal illustrations), *The Illustrated Guide to Viking Martial Arts* (internal illustrations), and *The Lost Warfare of India: An Illustrated Guide* (front cover designer).

ALSO FROM WATKINS

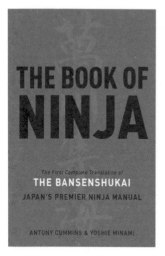

THE BOOK OF
NINJA

The First Complete Translation of
THE BANSENSHUKAI
JAPAN'S PREMIER NINJA MANUAL

ANTONY CUMMINS & YOSHIE MINAMI

THE BOOK OF NINJA

Known in Japanese as the *Bansenshūkai*, *The Book of Ninja* is the ultimate *ninjutsu* manual. It was written in 1676 by Fujibayashi Yasutake. Born in the post-civil war era of Japan, Fujibayashi-sensei collected and combined information from the clans of Iga and Kōka – the homelands of the ninja – and compiled it into an authoritative book, which has now been translated into English by the Historical *Ninjutsu* Research Team. It is widely considered to be the "bible" of *ninjutsu*, the art of the ninja. The Book of Ninja begins with an in-depth introduction to the history of Fujibayashi-sensei's scripture. Then the teachings themselves, appealingly rendered in this translation, take us into the secrets of guerrilla warfare and espionage. We learn how to become the ultimate spy, whether by building a network of spies or by hiding in plain sight. Through the stealth and concealment tactics of night-time infiltration and through weapon and tool building skills, as well as mission planning, we can learn much both about warfare and about adopting the right mindset for tackling our own inner and outer enemies. Adding to the mix for the spycraft lover, there are sections on capturing criminals, performing night raids, making secret codes and signs, and even techniques for predicting the weather and using an esoteric Buddhist system of divination. An exciting and engaging tome of lost knowledge, *The Book of Ninja* is the final say in the world of the ninja and the ultimate classic for samurai and ninja enthusiasts alike.

THE BOOK OF SAMURAI

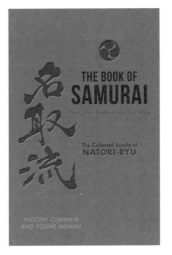

The Book of Samurai is a translation of two secret scrolls which establish the fundamental teachings of a samurai and ninja school known as Natori-Ryū. The first scroll, *Heika Jōdan*, contains 290 lessons which form a baseline of knowledge for samurai during times of peace, and focus each student to expand on their own ability and conduct, giving them the mindset needed for battles to come. The second scroll, Ippei Yōkō, moves the student onto the field of battle, giving them an understanding of what is expected of them during a campaign of war. These first two Natori-Ryū documents are an in-depth and detailed account of the practice of samurai warfare, opening up the lost world of these Japanese warriors to all modern readers.

Natori-Ryū originally closed its doors in 1868 after the fall of the samurai, but in 2013 the original Natori family gave Antony Cummins permission to re-establish the school based on the original scrolls and annotations left in multiple library collections. All are welcome to join in and study both the skills of the samurai and the auxiliary arts of the *shinobi* under the guidance of Natori-Ryū. Simply visit www.natori.co.uk and click Natori-Ryū.

WATKINS

Sharing Wisdom Since
1893

The story of Watkins began in 1893, when scholar of esotericism John Watkins founded our bookshop, inspired by the lament of his friend and teacher Madame Blavatsky that there was nowhere in London to buy books on mysticism, occultism or metaphysics. That moment marked the birth of Watkins, soon to become the publisher of many of the leading lights of spiritual literature, including Carl Jung, Rudolf Steiner, Alice Bailey and Chögyam Trungpa.

Today, the passion at Watkins Publishing for vigorous questioning is still resolute. Our stimulating and groundbreaking list ranges from ancient traditions and complementary medicine to the latest ideas about personal development, holistic wellbeing and consciousness exploration. We remain at the cutting edge, committed to publishing books that change lives.

DISCOVER MORE AT:
www.watkinspublishing.com

Read our blog

Watch and listen to
our authors in action

Sign up to
our mailing list

We celebrate conscious, passionate, wise and happy living.
Be part of that community by visiting

 /watkinspublishing   @watkinswisdom

/watkinsbooks   @watkinswisdom